We
Belong
Tae
Glasgow

Danny Gill

*Front cover photo: **Glasgow Cross taken by Alisdair Woodburn***

ISBN: 978-0-244-49089-8

PublishNation
www.publishnation.co.uk

Other books by Danny Gill which can be bought from Lulu.com and Amazon as either a paperback or a Kindle ebook.

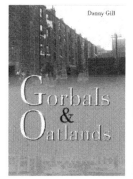
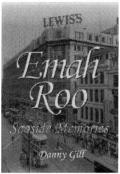

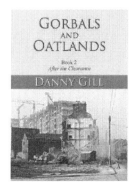

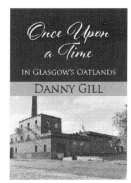

All proceeds from this book will be shared equally between:-

The upkeep of the Southern Necropolis Graveyard on Caledonia Road in the Gorbals area of Glasgow; and

The Benny Lynch statue campaign.

My sincerest thanks to everyone who purchases this book.

Danny Gill

Foreword

I have written this book for Glaswegians, wherever we are in this old world of ours. I have done my best in my research to give general information on Glasgow's fine buildings and some of its famous sons and daughters. I found out many things I never knew before about Glasgow [and some of its people] and was impressed as I hope you the reader are.

I have not shied away from the green/blue - blue/green divide in Glasgow and have tried to be very even-handed whilst doing this. If anyone thinks that I haven't, then all I can say is I done my best and say no more than that.

I have tried a new format with my poems in this book as in not only showing the poem but on the opposite page give a photo of the poem's subject with text underneath it giving more information.

I would have liked more of people's stories and asked for them on many face-book pages but only got a hand full back, so then I had to put my cap in hand and send out PM's to friends and was greatly surprised and thank-full that most of them did send me their stories about themselves in. Of course, I could have done with more people's stories but I realise that lots of people don't feel up to doing that and that is no problem at all, I fully understand.

So, I just enlarged the other chapters to give the book a decent page count of around or just over 200 pages which will fit snugly and comfy as a paperback in the reader's hand.

So, sit back folks and let's take a wander through Glasgow, its streets, buildings and people and, as someone once said, you can take the guy/girl out of Glasgow but you can never take Glasgow out of that person.

I left Glasgow 51 years ago as a young 20-year-old bricklayer to build bricks halfway round the world. I may have left Glasgow all those years ago, but Glasgow has certainly never left me. I do hope you enjoy it as much as I did when writing it.

Acknowledgements

First of all, I would like to thank Alisdair Woodburn for giving me the front cover photo for my book and ten photos in Chapter 8. You went out of your way big time to get me these photos and I will be eternally grateful to you for doing this.

I would also like to thank Carol Connolly for one of the internal photos in my book. Many thanks Carol. Also for other photos I would like to thank Glasgow city archives, Urban Glasgow, and the Evening times/Daily record newspapers, The Only Way Is Gorbals Facebook site. Full credit and thanks to you all.

Also, many thanks to the people who took the time to send me in the stories of their life and poems/jokes. I really am grateful to you all. There are quite a few people to name so forgive me for not naming you all, but you all know who you are and I truly am over the moon that you all helped me.

I would like to thank all those involved in the "Castlemilk history group." For their help, I have given a full list of acknowledgements and thanks at the end of my chapter about Castlemilk and different groups/individuals.

Also thanks to the people who I asked about certain matters about my book and they replied with great enthusiasm, which was a great relief.

Many thanks once again to David and Gwen Morrison, my publishers at PublishNation for giving me another first-class book to be proud of.

My sincerest thanks to all above and I hope that you the reader enjoys reading this book about our native Glasgow and her people.

Many thanks.
Danny Gill.
2019

*This book is dedicated to all Glaswegians
wherever you are in this old world of ours.*

*Glasgow is in our blood since the day we were born
until the day we die.*

*Some of the buildings may change
but Glaswegians never do.*

Contents

Chapter 1

Poems

The Whistling Kettle

Ma's kitchen had many things, tins of vim to bottles of Dettol.
But I know her her pride and joy was that auld whistling kettle.

She used it for oh so many chore's, carrying oot her daily toil.
The gas always kept on a peep so it wouldn't take long to boil.

When the kettle whistled alerting oor Ma's to their job in hand.
Like fillin up the hot water bottle, makin the bed warm n grand.

Her turn came round to wash the stairs, she done it withoot fail.
The whistlin kettle wae its boiling water filled up oor Ma's pail.

And as weans all hating that night for that auld tin bath of metal.
Waiting oor turn until Ma said, right you are next my wee petal.

Just a few jobs the Whistling Kettle done, I'm sure you'll agree.
But most important job was for wee Granny to make a pot o tea.

Today we have kitchens wae cordless kettles made out of plastic.
Wish we were living in the tenements when oor life wiz fantastic

Who can remember the auld whistling kettle that our Ma's used to always have on a peep on the gas stove. It really did do so many chores for us when we all lived in the tenements [maybe after the tenements too as people had got used to it]. Every tenement stair you climbed up you could hear that screech like a Banshee coming from behind the door and do you remember as a wean pulling the whistle stop off of the kettle and blowing into it? Of course times moved on and as we moved to new houses [mainly to the new housing schemes, people were starting to buy electric kettles and just look at the electric cordless kettles that we have today!!!!! Its funny how when we think back of things like the whistling kettle, the hot water bottle, hanging the front door key on a piece of string behind the door that remembers us of those days of long ago. We may now live in super dooper houses with all the mod cons but to me my memories of hame was living back in the tenements where we had that great close knit community spirit.

The Wedding Scramble

I think of an event of years ago, I explain it without preamble.
As one and all we got ready, for that Wedding Day scramble.

Bride and Groom jist newly married looked happy and sweet.
Covered in confetti, they went into the wedding car back seat.

Then as the car did edge away, the car windae it wound down.
As a handful of coins got chucked oot landing onto the ground.

All Hell broke loose as the coins got thrown, Oh whit a scatter.
Men, Wummin and weans aw dived in, sure age diddny matter.

Pushing and shovin and elbows used, trying for a penny or two.
Somebody got a broken finger and some poor wean lost a shoe.

The lucky wans who got a penny, went tae spend it in the shop.
Unlucky wans looked a Mess , as the one shoe wean did a hop.

Getting married and having a family its all part of life's gamble.
Not a patch as diving in heid first, at the wedding day scramble

How many of us remember getting skint knees and crushed fingers in the madcap melee of diving in head first at the wedding scramble, life was hard back then and yes every penny counted [that's why you had grown up women in the thick of it] if they could get threepence or sixpence it would go towards getting a meal on the table. The news of an impending wedding was in the air and people would gather from early morning in anticipation of the coins to be thrown out of the bride and grooms car and a big scream went up when the penny's, threepenny bits etc were thrown in the air as the car drove away. I know some people went regularly over the the Toon to Martha street registry office to try their luck [usually on a Saturday]. Sadly it seems to be a thing of the past just like the "Christening pieces" that were held to a boy or girl at the christening of a baby, if you remember the "Christening piece " was usually a buttered double digestive biscuit with a half crown piece [2/6d in old money] if the baby was a girl then the "Christening piece" was held to the first boy that the proud parents saw when coming out of the Church/Chapel and vice versa if the baby was a boy, it was held to the first girl. I tell my grandweans here in London about this and they look on in awe.

Paddy's Market

Paddy's Market wiz always packed, with a buzz always in the air.
In fact it got that busy ye'd swear blind half of Glasgow wiz there.

Gorbals folk walked over the Albert bridge, across the river Clyde.
All looking for a cheap bargain, as Glaswegians stood side by side.

There wiz old tin baths, second hand tools, laying there all asunder.
Old tackity boots and shoes wae nae laces, all for a tanner or under.

Old fur coats at a bargain price, old clothes piled up three feet high.
There wiz hardly anything in Paddy's Market that you coodny buy.

A cafe nearby selling ribs and cabbage or a big plate a stewed beef.
And a big mug of extra strong tea, wid strip the enamel aff yer teeth.

Then Glasgow City Council shut Paddy's Market , we were so irate.
Just as well we still have the Barras a wee bit alang the Gallowgate.

And although Paddy's Market has gone, we remember it wae pride.
Because many a bargain went hame wae us in Glasgow far and wide

How many of us can recall Paddy's market. As I said in my poem on the opposite page it was always packed as the photo above shows. For me coming from the Gorbals / Oatlands area in the soo side it was just a walk away and how I loved going there as a wean. Of course some people would "turn their noses up" at the mention of Paddy's market but remember back in those far off days money was very hard to come by and every penny counted so bargain hunting oor Ma's and wee Granny's went!!! You could literally buy anything [including the kitchen sink] for example in the photo above you can see a lawnmower up for sale, there were old shovels and golf bags with golf clubs in them, prams and an eternal amount of old clothes and shoes at cheap prices. Only drawback sometimes was the "smell" and oh yes because it was underneath the railway arches you did have some rats scurrying around but most people there were oblivious to this "downside" of Paddy's market and to me it added to the buzz of being there. We all have our memories of Paddy's market and mine were of having a good old "nose" around looking at everything on sale, although as a wean I would never buy anything but it was just the excitement of being there. Of course if my Ma and Granny took me there they would always buy something and they always seemed to meet people that they knew, yes it was a great place to meet old faces. Such a shame its closed now.

<u>Windae Hingin</u>

Remember the Glasgow of years ago, in my memory I do dredge.
I can see my Ma and Granny , all leaning on their Windae Ledge.

Glaswegians called it this as we spoke to oor neighbour next door.
With a pillow or cushion under their elbows, in case they got sore.

Chatted to your pals either side, ye'd hear all about peoples capers.
News got passed by word of mouth eh who needed the newspapers.

Ye always faced into the street when you done your windae hingin.
No from the back windae cos the smell o the middens were mingin.

Watching the drunks comin oot the pub, they held us all in a trance.
With a fish supper in wan poacket, they'd sing and gave us a dance.

Then a wumman from across the street, started making a big racket.
Shouting down aw that's my man, hope he still has his wage packet.

The tenements got demolished, replaced with buildings very dreamy.
Windae hingin's a thing of the past noo, jist like gaun to the Steamie.

I remember with great fondness my Ma and my wee granny doing their windae hingin, this goes back to the days of the old tenements when there were no televisions [well perhaps into the mid to late 1950's before people really started getting tv's in their houses.] or mobile phones or laptops/computers that we all take for granted nowadays and to get the local news and "gossip", news was passed by word of mouth from neighbours doing their windae hingin. Also back in the days of the tenements the windae hingers would keep a close eye on all of us weans who were playing in the street below to make sure we were all safe. While shouting down a word of warning if some bigger wean was taking "liberties" with younger weans as in snatching their sweeties etc. I used to sit sometimes beside my Ma or Granny and we would look down into the streets below, it was such a great feeling of a very close knit community, where we all knew each other. We might not have had much money but what we had we shared and us weans were loved unconditionally.

Dizzy Corner [Dissy corner]

Many's a place in Glesga, where young lovers decided to meet.
But none so famous as "Dizzy Corner" at Argyle /Union street.

Young Romantics from every district, headed over to the Toon.
To stand beneath Boot's clock, hoping they widdny be let doon.

The lassie was standing there aw dressed up like a "dugs dinner".
For the guy that she met at the dancing sure looked like a winner.

Ten feet away stood this guy who kept getting redder in the face.
What if his burd never turned up, man that would be a Disgrace.

But the time was now almost eight o'clock , both were in a tizzy.
Cause they knew within their hearts both had been given a dizzy.

Getting a dizzy at Boots corner, made it never a nice place to be.
I know what I am talking about as it happened three times to me.

This all happened in my younger days, I wiz slim wae lots a hair.
Today I only get a dizzy gettin up too quick fae my rocking chair.

Yes the famous or infamous "Dizzy corner" at the corner of Argyle street and Union street in Glasgow town centre. Actually it was originally named "Disappointment corner" for obvious reasons but then this was shortened to "Dissy corner" and later pronounced as "Dizzy corner" but whether you got a "Dissy" or a "Dizzy" it still never made you feel good. My story was one night when I was 20 years old I was bragging to all my other bricklayer mates at work how I was meeting a beautiful girl called Cathy there that night at 7 o'clock. I finished work early at 4'clock that day, went home had a bath, dressed up in my best suit and what happened it was 8 o'clock and I was standing there , no sign of Cathy and all my workmates passed by in the building site bus that took us to work, oh yes they saw me and started shouting Danny's got a Dizzy. Oh the Shame!!!!

Chapter2

People's stories

Patricia Docherty

I would like to tell you a wee story about my late grandmother Mary who lived in the maisonettes in Hutchensontown Court in the Gorbals. She was a regular customer at the Phoenix public house nearby. They called her Mary "the Boomerang"because when she was worse for wear due to the whisky then a member of the bar staff would take her to her home, make sure she was safe in her house, then lock the door and post her keys through the letterbox. Within fifteen minutes she "escaped" and was once more back in the pub hence the nickname "Boomerang Mary".

One story about one of my granny's "escapes" actually happened when I was on my first date with with my now husband David. It was a summers night about 9,30 pm and myself and David were sitting on a wall of a grass verge outside of my granny's kitchen window and our first date was almost over. My granny's kitchen window opened very slowly, a handbag was thrown out of the window and two feet appeared, followed by legs, it was my granny "escaping" back to the Phoenix pub. Margaret McGuigan Bonner who worked in the Phoenix had taken her home, locked the door and posted the keys through the letterbox as was the normal.

My granny was that drunk she couldn't find the keys and this was why she was "escaping" from her house via the kitchen window. Well David shouted out "Oh my God, look at that wee wummin dreeping out of that window". Luckily enough she lived on the ground floor but the window was quite high up. I couldn't move for laughing, I didn't know whether to laugh or greet so I turned round to David and said "now you have met my granny, do you still want to go out with me ?

This was just one of the stories in regards to my granny "Boomerang Mary" and her trips to the Phoenix public house.

PS Sadly, Patricia who gave me this story, has passed away. R.I.P Tricia. X

Norrie McNamee

My name is Norman McNamee, born 1945 Pembroke South Wales, my Scots father met my Welsh mother on a Lincoln air base during WW2.

After my father was demobbed,1946, I was brought to the north end of Glasgow in Possilpark, to stay with my grandparents in Mansion St, later on we moved to Huntershill St Springburn. In 1947 there were 4 of us, my sister was born in late 1947, 4 of us in a single end, cold water flat, gas lighting, coal for heat and the oven for cooking, we may have had a gas-ring, while sharing an outside toilet with 3 other families.

My first school was Elmvale Primary, Hawthorn St, Springburn, as kids we didn't know we were living in poor conditions.

We moved in 1953 to a brand new flat in Milton, Shapinsay St. Oh what luxury!! A bedroom each for my sister and I, a living room, a bathroom and a kitchen, heated by coal and we had electricity too.

I attended Elmvale for a year or so till the new school was made ready for us, Elmvale primary, Scalpay st, Milton.

When I was 12 years old I went to Colston Secondary school, Springburn rd, I must mention apart for my first day at school and being bussed from Milton to Elmvale, I walked to school, there and back every day.

I Left school June 1960 and started work on 1st August with A&J Main, structural engineers at Hawthorn st, Possilpark where I served an Apprenticeship as a Template Maker, I left Mains in 1967 and married Claire in September of that year and started work with Clyde Structural, South st Scotstoun, we bought a room and kitchen in Henrietta st, Scotstoun around the corner from Clyde Structural.

Left Clyde Structural to return to A & J Main 1968??? only to find out after the Glasgow Fair that Mains was closing, so I moved to Bairds of Anniesland Structural Engineers, stayed for 8 months and moved back to Clyde Structural 1969 where I remained till 1972, having worked in the Template Loft and design and estimating dept that didnt work out too well.

I got the sack for making a mistake, managed to get back into Template Loft before being paid off again for a trivial mistake. turns out my card was marked as one of the directors wasn't too happy that I managed to get back into the Template Loft, on hindsight I may have been too young for the design Dept, head full of nonsense!!

In between all that I had passed my driving test 15th December 1970 first time, we got a car so we moved to East Kilbride 1971, Saddlers Well court Calderwood, High Rise stayed there for a year or so and moved to a ground floor flat in Shira Terrace Calderwood, stayed there till 1974.

Back to being laid off, 10 days on the dole after being sacked from Clyde Structural, my pals dad got me a job as a Joiner, I said to him I am a Template Maker not a joiner, he said but you can use a chisel, hammer and saw? So there I was working as Joiner for Gilchrist's of Barrland st, in folks houses, Police Stations and buildings sites etc, 4 old penny's over the union rate to boot, I enjoyed that job, dirty at times hard work often but I did learn a lot which stood me in good stead for jobs around the house and helping friends with alterations to their house and garage.

I left Gilchrist's after 8 months, 1973, and went to work for Lambhill Engineering Strachur st, A former neighbour who had heard I was out of work but I wasn't, contacted me and asked if I wanted to come back into my trade, so I worked there for 8 months, pattern emerging? no, just coincidence.

August 1974, I started the best job I ever had, Babcock and Wilcox, out at Renfrew.

Our title was Process Engineers, full staff conditions, we used a coding system for making Templates, no wood used and paper for smaller templates.

The job involved us working out rates for Steel preparation, Welding and Fabrication, Quality Control, and being introduced to a PC to input or data for the Rates a wee,bit more involved than making wooden Templates but I loved that job.

I always said they would have to throw me out of Babcock's come September 1993 that's what happened the day before we went to visit my aunts in Canada and USA.

4 months on the dole, January 1994, I got word I had been accepted for a position as a Concierge in the Gorbals at Norfolk Court , Gorbals cross.

Massive change to my life, dropped a bit of money but I was glad to be working, I was 48, my working partner (we worked in 2 man teams) was 25, the old yin and the young yin.

A learning curve, security, CCTV duties, cleaning the stairs, the site, rotating bins, dealing with public, biting your tongue, recording incidents, repairs, dealing with Police Fire and Ambulance services, Housing Officers, handing out keys to Home Helps, helping tenants back into their house after being locked out, joinery came in handy, going to court as witnesses for various crimes including Murder, as I said, a learning curve and learn we did.

I took early retirement when I was 61, one of our Concierge's a few months older than me died when I was 60, it ate away at me, I didn't want to die in the job, I soldiered on but went on the sick, my wife said she thought I was under stress as did a neighbour, my doctor gave me my first sick line, Glasgow City Housing tried to help me with counselling, offers of other jobs but after nearing the point of getting no wages I said lets wrap this up I want to retire and I did at 61, am still sometimes in denial about being stressed but it was the best thing I ever done.

Perhaps if I wasn't pensioned, 23 years in the service (paid 19 years Babcock Pension into Council scheme and 1 for 23 years for it) I might have toughed it out, glad I didn't.

While in Babcock's I got into taking photos of Glasgow and after working in the Gorbals I got interested in the history of Oatlands as well and am still taking shots of Glasgow and areas.

I have donated to The Mitchell Library 12 DVDs containing thousands of shots taken in Glasgow, the tenements and City Centre, I am working on 5 more, nowadays the shots I take are of the changes to Glasgow of what's coming down and what's going up, keeps me busy, I hill walk as well I have seen more of Scotland since I took up that hobby, its nearly 20 years I have been walking, I take shots of all our walks.

Authors note: A great big thanks to you Norrie for helping me over the years with supplying me your photos for my books, Thanks pal.

Irene [Donna] Robertson

Lived up a dunny close wae a gas light in Fordneuk st Brigton... with ma auntie Eva and her man ma uncle Matt ma mammy and daddy as a hid thought for years... wee room and kitchen wae odd furniture...waxcloth on the flerr, varnished panelled doors. inset beds and formica roon the sink when we went upmarket in the 50s.... we even got a chrome well wae H on it but no a drap of hot watter came oot it. Then we got an Imp cream cooker.. two rings, a wee grill and oven.. and a place fur the pots at the bottom... it sat in an old press near the sink that the door hid been took aff.. and ma mammy hid put congowall tiled cloth stuff roon the back for splashes.....She wiz always polishing the waxcloth and a wiz always fawing and bangin ma heid.. but she thote her wee hoose wiz lovely and it was.... it was home..... Funny but in those days ye paid up stuff before ye got it instead of HP... she wiz always up at Jacks the furniture shop at Parkhead paying up a set of drawers or a new interior sprung bed.... wonder how many remember them....it wiz a massive heavy spring in a widdin surround that sat on metal things against the recess walls.. then the mattress went on tap.... She did though go tae Fishers warehouse as well for stuff .. think everyone did back then and the man came to the hoose every Friday for payments.........OH aye and the meter man for the gas ....pennies fae heaven efter hed emptied the meter..........hed put aw the big pennies in wee piles and coont them then gie ye back a rebate...............I always got wan wee pile to maself...

The one person I hated coming to the door wiz the schoolboard man...... a wiz aff a lot when younger wae illnesses and ma auntie wid tell me tae run intae the room and kid a wiz sleeping if he came as they were awfy strict... ye wurnae allowed to look ok or be sitting up.... so that got me aw stressed hivving tae hide.... Funny how smells stick in yer heid and make ye remember things fae the past........a always mind Pine tabs.. a bar of this stuff like set jelly ye put in the pail to wash the sterrs.....oh a loved that smell and wid stick ma heid in the bucket wae the steam rising tae sniff it...then watch ma mammy breaking up pipeclay and putting it intae the pail anaw to wash the sterrs.nae mops back then. wid hiv been a riddy to be caught using a mop fur the sterrs.. doon on yer hauns and knees wae a scrubber.. nae wonder the women aw hid swollen bad knees.. and if ye stood on the sterrs while they were getting washed ye wid get walloped roon the legs wae the wet cloth...

Another smell a loved wiz when the Betterwear man came tae the door wae his big case.... he always hid Lavender polish in a big tin and he wid gie me a wee tiny tin of it as a gift....he wid take orders for brushes and stuff and deliver them a couple of weeks later... good quality stuff anaw...

Pat Hughes

I was born in Pettigrew street, Shettleson, Glasgow in 1940. My mum was Irish, however she was brought up in the Gorbals. My dad was from Townhead, Glasgow.

When they got married they stayed in Sandyfaulds lane/street in the Gorbals. My mum's dad, my grandfather had a horse and cart with a stable in Sandyfaulds lane and rented his horse and carts to scrap men and coalmen. His sons took buckets of kindling sticks to the Gorbals and his daughters sold fruit and veg.

My mum had 4 daughters, all born in the Gorbals then they moved us out to Shettleson due to overcrowding and this is when she had her first boy, me, followed by 3 other boys.

My oldest sister suffered with TB and went out with Tommy Doherty the Celtic player who later went on to become manager of Manchester united football club. Due to her condition we got a new house in Hapland rd, Pollok, Glasgow. Unfortunately she passed away in 1950 at only 20 years old and my mother died shortly after in 1953 at 47 years of age. My other 3 sisters were married and moved into their own homes across Glasgow. My dad was a labourer in the ship yards for his whole life, being left with 4 young boys all still at school.

We were moved to Middleton street near Ibrox, Glasgow, at 16, I moved in with my sister in Camden street Gorbals until 1957 when I joined the army. I still stayed with her in the Gorbals when I returned home on leave and met my first wife Sandra McNair in the Gorbals. Sandra's father was a docker and came from Waddell street in the Gorbals. We married in 1959.

When I finished in the army my sister had moved to Carnoustie street, Kinning park, Glasgow and I had just got a house off of Scotland street with Sandra. Together we had a daughter, Lynn who is now 57 and a son Patrick who unfortunately died at only a few days old. For various reasons the marriage did not work out and I moved to Carnoustie street to my sister.

I later met my second wife, Margaret McCourt around a year later from Lawmoor street Gorbals. Together we got a house on Caledonia rd. We had 2 sons, Patrick [born in 1967] and Gerald 18 months later. We were one of the last buildings in the Gorbals with an indoor toilet. They began pulling down the Gorbals and we got a maisonette on McNeil street, I was a lorry driver, taxi driver, labourer and bus driver and worked for Dunn and Moore until in 1972 I took over the "Popinjay" pub in Stockwell street Glasgow. Within a year I bought the pub from the landlord and changed the name to "The Wee Mann's Bar" which I owned for around 10 years.

Following this I moved to Dumfries and ran a pub which was in the family for around 20 years with my eldest son Patrick taking it over from me. I moved into the catering trade running hamburger vans and had a take away cafe called "The Waterfront Takeaway". Patrick bought this from me when I retired to look after Margaret. Unfortunately Margaret passed away in January of 2016. I was her carer for 7 years due to her spinal problems and gave up my football to spend all my time with her.

I have now taken my season pass back out as she had instructed me to do, and make sure to go up for as many games as possible.

Stories from the pub

Shortly after I took the pub over, Thursday was "Top of the Pops" night and a crowd of bikers came in from the Scotia across the road. They were all carrying their own bottles of Newcastle Brown ale and turned my TV over to "Top of the Pops". I asked our waitress Jean what was going on as our other customers were already watching another channel. I unplugged the TV set, at which time they started cursing at me claiming that I was going to lose them as good customers, although they were not spending any money. Jean explained that they came in every week and did this but they had always been too afraid to say anything to them, they left and never came back again.

Sinky

Sinky worked for Bernard Corrigan the fishmonger, he was an alcoholic. Bernard would employ him, then sack him for something but take him back again. Now off the drink you could not meet a nicer chap. He was very educated, smart and friendly, he would get on with everyone and regularly chatted to Billy Connolly in the "Wee Mann's Pub" and you would hear the two of them talking and making jokes. Sinky was a very funny man who would have you laughing for hours.

The first story I heard about Sinky when he began drinking in my pub was that he was a "Peterman" who would open a safe during a robbery. Across from the pub there was a big sailing boat called "The Carrick" which was used for for a private club for the RNVA. There were 2 shops there, one was a bakery and the other was a Catholic shop selling Catholic merchandise. It was coming up to a bank holiday and the bakery was to be closed for the long weekend.two men approached Sinky to break into the safe in the bakery. In order to get to the safe of the bakery they they would first have to get into the Catholic shop and go through the basement, halfway through the job the battery in their torch died. One of the men behind the plan offered to go for batteries but Sinky refused as it was too risky. Sinky looked around for ideas and saw a full size Virgin Mary statue which he brought over to where they were working, he took the baby Jesus statue out of the Virgin Mary's arms and put candles it the hands of the Virgin Mary while exclaiming "Forgive me for my sins " and carried on breaking the wall through the basement. This is only hearsay, however it was backed up by Bernard who was an honest man.

When Sinky hit the drink he was barred from all the pubs in the area including "The wee Mann's bar". He was staying with his sister who put him out for his drinking and went to the "Men's Model" on Duke street in Dennistoun, Glasgow. He had no money and was put out of the model but his sister wouldn't take him back in unless he gave up the drink. Everyone in the pub had bets on as to whether he would end up in jail for Christmas and New year as he did every year. There was a law out at the time when "Petermen" would get jail for being caught with a screwdriver [we'll come back to this].

Sinky wanted to go to the jail as he had nowhere else to stay, so at 8 pm one night he went to Glasgow cross and put a brick through the window of an electrical shop and stood waiting for the police to turn up but they didn't!! After waiting for so long he filled his pockets with tape recorders, radios and anything else he could carry.

Around shutting time at "The wee Mann's pub" he came in asking for a carry out, I told him that he was barred and had no money. He told me that he had done a good job and had enough money to stay at the model for a month and asked for two bottles of cheap wine and some beer. I decided to let him have it and he told me that he would go back to the model and would be off the drink by the New Year. He went off up the High street to book himself into the men's model, he was nearly there when two policemen stopped him and asked to see what was in his bag and found the carry out. They also found a screwdriver and was automatically sent to jail, he had stood for ages waiting to get arrested and couldn't get the jail, then he finally had the money to sort himself out and instantly got 3 months in jail.

He was off the drink for a long time and met a lady at an AA meeting, he began working for me collecting tumblers and cleaning the cellar, after about 3 months of him being off the drink I gave him a fiver to grab me a fish supper as I couldn't get away from the pub. A few hours later I went looking for him, a customer saw me and asked if I was looking for Sinky. We found him up a close with chips and a bottle of wine, I asked him what he was doing as he took my banking for me regularly and never touched a penny but as soon as had a fiver he bought drink. He told me that if he touched the banking money I'd have thrown him in the river Clyde but surely I wouldn't hit him for a fiver. That was him back on the drink!!

Pat Belton

I was told he was a great guy until he was sent to the Navy as a young man in WW2. He went out to collect the bodies from blown up ships around the English coast. He had a trade at one time I believe but unfortunately the drink cost him his job, him and his wife were both drinkers and he worked part time in the market. He was never a problem but his wife argued regularly.

One day he went home with some fish from the market looking forward to the bottle of wine he had hidden at home. He found his wife sitting with the empty bottle of wine saying she had found it in the house. He was so angry that he hit her with the bag of fish. She called the police and he was taken to jail. Margaret my wife was very fond of Pat and asked me to see if I could get him out on bail. I told her that he would be going to court but I would go to the hearing. He was in front of a very strict Sherrif, Sherrif Longmuir was his name and he regularly drank in "Bells bar" and also liked the wine but was very strict on people who mistreated their wife. He asked Pat why he had hit his wife with a bag of fish, Pat responded by saying that he was "putting her in her plaice".

He was given 30 days for contempt of court and got no time for hitting his wife.

One day, after hours we had 2 cops in the bar. One from Yorkshire called Brian and the other called Ian from Glasgow. They got a call to go to Pat's house for a family conflict, Brian took the call and agreed to attend. He then turned to Ian and said he didn't want to go.

Pat lived 4 stories high up in the flats, he said "we'll get to the door, she'll be crying and she'll tell us that she doesn't want him arrested but just to give him a fright, what does she think we are bloody ghosts".

Gunboat Smith

When I met this guy he was in his late 70's and I had assumed he had been in the war. We had a war hero called Jimmy who was a regular in the pub but he never talked about his time in the war. Jimmy asked Gunboat Smith what he had done in the war, he told him that once he was running along the grass and ran into a German who pulled out a small pistol, all he had was a small knife. He swiped the knife out and the German mocked him saying that he'd missed. Gunboat warned him not to shake his head! I asked gunboat what he actually did in the Navy and he told me he was actually in jail for 3 years in Barlinnie!!

He had been in a pub in Duke street with his girlfriend, he went to the toilets and returned to a sailor with his arm around his girlfriend trying to buy her a drink.

He smashed a glass in the sailor's face and was sent to jail. The nickname Gunboat Smith was given to him during his time in jail and stuck with him ever since.

Authors note: I met up with Pat Hughes one day in the Clutha bar as I was up from London on my yearly holiday back hame and I was meeting up with friends when he kindly agreed to give me this story. Actually Pat had read on one of the Gorbals face-book pages that I was meeting up with pals that day and as he was in Glasgow that day he kindly went out of his way to come into the Clutha to see me.

There was quite a crowd of pals who came to meet me that day in the Clutha and I was trying to give everyone a chance to speak to me [and me to them], so I could only speak to Pat for a short while.

Also may I say that my company and me all had a great day, I got to see pals that I hadn't seen in a year or two and the beer was flowing fast and so too were the story's and laughs.

Elizabeth Evans

I was born in 1958 in Cornwall street, Kinning Park and shortly after that we moved to Tradeston, to a 'pen' in Dalintober street. We remained there for a few years after which, we moved just around the corner to 241 Wallace street, where I mostly grew up, until I was 21 years old!

I'm an only child and I had a very happy childhood but I must admit I always longed for a brother or a sister.

My dad, Bobby Evans, was a bricklayer and then a slater later on. He was the happiest of men, always a smile on his face and a song in his heart and he always whistled all the tunes he knew, all day long.

He taught me how to read and write at a very young age and we had a great relationship, going for long walks together with my doll's pram, often to Maxwell Park in 'The Shields', up the road from where we lived.

I remember really clearly, one day in particular at Maxwell Park during Autumn. The large pond was partially covered with the fallen leaves and I didn't realise this and stepped on to the leaves, only to find myself up to my neck in the water, completely soaked! My dad fished me out and wheeled me home, in my doll's pram, which fortunately was a Silver Cross Twin pram so I was warm and cosy until we got home!

We had many 'adventures' together and I remember them as though they took place yesterday.

My mum, Sarah, was much more reserved and she stayed at home until I was 8 years old when she took a part-time job as a Supervisor at the Rowntree – Mackintosh factory in the nearby Stanley Street. I became the envy of all my schoolmates because every week we got loads of biscuits, sweets and chocolate from the factory shop but I always shared everything with them, that was my nature, just like my dad!

I loved playing in our street with all my pals, the street was always full of kids. We girls mostly played with balls, ropes or at hide and seek or shops. We were so creative in our street games and we were never bored and never wanted to go home at teatime because we enjoyed ourselves so much.

I was in the Brownies and then the girl guides for some time and our meetings were at the big church in Pollok street. Some people frowned upon this because I was a Roman Catholic and most of the others were Protestants who were also members of the Pollok street church. I never cared about these differences because my mum's family were Church of England and my dad's were RC so I grew up with a very open mind concerning religion. Of course we were and still are Celtic supporters but my cousins on my mum's side were Rangers fans but we didn't let this come between us and respected each other's views.

My Primary school was Our Lady and St. Margaret's in Stanley street, next to our Parish Church where I sang in the Choir. I met my lifelong friend Elaine Ferrie on my first day at school, to be precise, at the infant's school which was in Admiral street. We were in the choir together, we went swimming at the swimming baths in Scotland street and every week, we went together to the hot baths in Tradeston, since we only had a toilet but no bath in our houses.

My Secondary school was St. Gerrard's in Govan, where I had many happy years and here I had the opportunity to meet new friends from other areas.

I played in the school hockey team and I played Netball for The Harmony Row Youth Club Team in Govan. I was in the debating society at St. Gerrard's and I started studying Italian at my school when I was about 14.

This was an unusual choice of subject at the time but I was curious and I loved languages.

I left school in 1974 and I went to the Sumlock college to become a Comptometer Operator, this was basically a manual calculator and when I finished my course, I worked for a couple of years with an important accountancy firm, with the auditors, travelling around the country, doing the audit in a variety of companies. I loved the travelling aspect of the job but I decided to go to college to continue studying languages, this was my desire deep down.

I went to Langside college and studied English, French, Italian, Spanish, History and Biology to Higher level. Not long before my final exams, I met my future husband at a college disco, an Italian boy who was studying English and working at The Malmaison Restaurant which was a very exclusive restaurant, owned by British Rail. It was located at the side of Glasgow Central Station, in Oswald street. (Not sure of the street name)

We very quickly fell in love, got married and our first house together was on a new housing estate called Park Gate in Govan!

However, in 1984, when our eldest daughter was three years old, we moved to his home town on the Adriatic coast. Thirty five years, three kids and two grandchildren later, we're still there, living very simply and happily together!

I've been teaching English for the past 33 years and teacher training for the past 10 years. I also work with a publisher of English Language Teaching material and have done so since 2001, as a language consultant and author. I love my life but I still go back to Glasgow every three months or so to visit my mum who's been living in Pollokshields since 1980. Sadly my dad passed away in 1989 but he managed to see all three of my kids and his memory lives on in all of us!

I was born on a Thursday and I've always believed the old rhyme … 'Thursday child has far to go'… I have come far, from my beginnings in Kinning Park but my past has made me into the person I am today, I will never forget where I came from, Good old Glasgow, My dear Green City!

Jane Hardie Robertson

"My name is Jane Robertson. I was born Jane Cameron Mullin Hardie on the 26th June 1933 at 12 Seath Street, Govanhill. On the 25th March 1957 I married William Fraser Robertson at Martha Street Registry Office. After the service we went back to the Cockatoo Bar at Eglinton Toll for drinks with friends.

That evening my new husband and I went into town to see 'Babes In The Wood' at the Alhambra Theatre in Waterloo Street starring Jimmy Logan, Rikki Fulton and Kenneth McKellar. My husband had booked us a box ans as we were climbing the stairs towards it we bumped into Jimmy Logan backstage and my husband told him we were newly weds. During the show Jimmy Logan asked for the lights to be shone on the box where "there was a wee bride". I waved to the crowd like the Queen as they applauded.

About a year later we had moved to a wee house in Kilmarnock where my husband had got a new signalman's job at Kilmarnock No.1 signal box. One day I was talking to my neighbour and we got on the subject of Glasgow. She told me she rarely visited Glasgow but her and a group of friends had visited last year to see a Jimmy Logan show. I asked her what one and after checking with her husband, she replied it had been last March at the Alhambra. She remembered Jimmy Logan pointing out a wee bride up in a box and I told her that wee bride was myself!

Many, many years later, just before I retired, I worked for Glasgow City Council Museums Department and I ran the wee gift shop in Pollok House in the Pollok Park. One day while my head was down, I heard a well spoken voice talking about some of the stuff for sale and another voice calling him Ritchie. I looked up and found myself face to face with the legendary Rikki Fulton at my shop! I told him it was great to meet him but before he left, I told him how I saw him and Jimmy Logan at the Alhambra on my wedding night all those years ago."

A wee photo of Pollok house where Jane worked.

Catherine Glen

My Mum was born and brought up in Adelphi Street, in the Gorbals. However, although her childhood was happy, loved, surrounded and supported by a large second and third generation Irish family, she was determined to move away from the truly dreadful, grievously substandard, squalid, overcrowded housing situation; no regular fixed income, grinding poverty, no social security, just the Parish – a harsh, means testing judge. Adelphi Mansions, Aunt Rose said was the address, when her date asked to walk her home.

Number 134 was no upper class "wally" close but it was the scene of the vivid and, as yet, unfettered, imagination of childhood, that of Mary, my Mum, when she was a little girl, in the 1920s. She loved to dance and sing – all through adulthood, she wished that she'd had a lovely singing voice, instead of the very ordinary one she had. The close became her theatre, her stage.....and her make up box!! She would jump, as high as she could, to reach up and brush her hand against the limewash; dabbing it on her cheeks as face powder!! Then she'd sing and dance, as we say today, like no one was watching or listening, as only children – no matter where they're raised – can. She also used the powdery limewash to make her face so very, very pale; she hoped & believed if she lay down and stayed still long enough, her parents would think her dead!!! All that to get out of eating porridge, it never worked!!

In fact, Mum would not accept Dad's proposal of marriage unless they bought a house – where did that come from??!! No-one in her life had ever bought a house – but, upon their marriage in April 1939, Mum and Dad did just that, living in that self-same house for one year short of fifty, upon their deaths in 1988.

They set up home, still on the South side, a few miles outside the city boundary, which was at Muirend, in Stamperland, Clarkston. So far away from her childhood home that it was an area to which they would take the tram for a day out! There was a working farm at Muirend in my lifetime, it later became Safeway, the first American style supermarket in the vicinity. Next to that, stood the Toledo, our local cinema. Many a happy Saturday morning was spent there, as part of the Minors.

We went ice skating at Crossmyloof; we went horse riding in Busby, Mum and Dad were determined that we should try anything that we fancied, as they never really had. I attended ballet & dance classes in Clarkston Hall – I recall that the examiner remarked, on my first dance exam pass certificate "A very pleasing fairy", high praise, indeed for my mime!! Best of all, we had a caravan at Culzean Castle – such a perfect childhood playground, Mum's had been Glasgow Green, we were so very, very lucky. I certainly was aware of our good fortune, as I knew so much of Mum's childhood from me, at bedtime, saying "tell me about when you were wee", instead of her reading me a story. I was fascinated!

We were taken to the theatre, to the ballet, to musicals, I saw Betty Grable in Mame!! We often went to the live TV recording of The One O'Clock Gang, we saw pantomime and ice shows and there was always the old favourite, Kelvingrove Art Gallery & Museum, to see, again and again, the magnificent Christ of St John of the Cross painting, by Salvador Dali. I no longer live in Scotland but the last time I was "home" went back to see that painting, as I usually do.

I'm not boasting or bragging, I'm certain that parents always do their very best for their children, improving on what they, themselves had, what I am doing, is, even thirty years after her death, marvelling at my intrepid and remarkable Mum.

From where did she get the love of theatre and live shows?

From her childhood imagination, when she was the eldest of only three or four children, rather than the nine it ended up as?

I've often wondered what would these nine ordinary – but remarkable to me – people have done in this life had they been offered the same opportunities that I was; but that will always be one of life's "what ifs", we'll never know.

Primary school was Nissen huts and a couple of kind of portacabin on stilts classrooms sort of attached to our local church, both going by the name of St Joseph's, Clarkston. We used to walk down to the Rowallan Hall, nearer to Clarkston Toll, it became our dinner school. In the mid-sixties, we moved up the road to Sheddens, where a brand-new school had been built for us, complete with kitchen and dining room! The poor old church was demolished and replaced by a huge, white, fan-shaped edifice, a hideous thing!!

We, again, were so very lucky; I already knew some of the teachers since my older brother had attended St Jo's before I did and one of his best friends was the son of our favourite, Mrs Tomasso. Her brother-in-law was none other than Larry Marshall, the host of the One O'Clock Gang on TV and her husband was a local postman. We curtsied, boys saluted to the headmaster or the priest, whenever either of them came into our class, we all knew one another and new pupils, of which we had a few over the years, were readily made welcome – and, with our own kitchen making lunches – we no longer had tepid, lumpy custard, or cabbage that looked like soggy Izal medicated toilet paper!!! We played ball against the wall, Chinese ropes, endless skipping games and hand clapping games too. One of the best things was making a slide in the ice and snow – over the course of just two playtimes and one lunchtime, it would end up like glass and be super smooth and slippy.

We never fell from sliding and no, they never did close the school due to inclement weather!!

As did all but three or four of our primary seven class, with its forty or so pupils, we passed our "Quali", our Eleven Plus exam, so we were secure in further education and headed for senior, rather than junior, secondary school. What an adventure, I thought, having read every Enid Blyton book there was about Claudine or the Twins at St Clare's.

Absolute culture shock!!!!

Having had to apply for an extra special travel pass, for our red buses to take us over the city boundary, was the very least of it, timetables were a further trauma!!

Holyrood Senior Secondary school was enormous, it seems to house thousands and cover many miles. The "main building" was in Dixon Avenue, however, as first year girls, we were walked across and down to Polmadie, to the girls' annexe, a dirty, Gothic sandstone building, that boasted outside toilets and a gym hall that doubled as dining room. Regardless of which mode it was in, it never did smell good.

All of a sudden, we didn't know anyone, thrown in as we were with pupils from the Kings Park, Shawlands and Cathcart areas - Holyrood had such a wide catchment area as the only Catholic secondary school for miles around – besides Charlotte Street and Notre Dame, a bit uppity, as we thought they were - the pupils from the aforementioned areas were ok, just a bit less naïve than we were – I say "we", it may well just have been me – along with pupils from St Bonaventure's, which was "down the road", that is to say, from what we thought to be a pretty rough area. They seemed as hard as nails, with their self-imposed uniform of identical feathered haircuts and "shiner" jackets. They even wore make up – white, brilliantly shiny highlighter under their over-plucked eyebrows and a similarly pale, shiny product on their cheeks. Trying so hard to be different, yet all identical to one another.

We had all been to Campbell's in Victoria Road for the proper uniform, some of us even had a beret, with the school badge, bearing the motto "In Hoc Signo Vince" – in this sign, conquer! The sign being the cross of Jesus' crucifixion, Holyrood meaning, Holy Cross. Not a very Christian motto at all!! The school hymn was just as violent, penned, I believe, by the most delightful teacher in all of Holyrood, Mr Harvey, he taught English & geography and played the organ in church.

Come let us with glad music, extol our Holyrood!
Tis our especial glory, exalt we in the good!
For by the cross we triumph, our foe men we destroy!
Its standard is our signal, for victory and joy!!

The berets didn't last a term, our gaberdine trench coats and uniform school blazer, were very soon replaced by duffle coats and our school bags were usurped by a kind of navy carrier bag type thing, from M&S – the ultimate irony, surely!!

I hated maths and the teacher, I hated arithmetic and the teacher – he used to throw the wooden and felt blackboard duster at anyone not paying attention – with unerring accuracy, the felt part quite deliberately well chalked – neither funny, big nor clever, our uniforms were navy blue. Bully!! Latin classes were presided over by Mrs Forrester, we had to behave then, she pitched up at St Joseph's for Sunday Mass, with her umpteen children, in a Volkswagen Camper van, the only vehicle that would take all of them!!

All the others had had some basic French lessons, via television in school, we were at a disadvantage.

Miss Murray, young as she was, in those swinging sixties, of the tangerine two piece, the impeccable shampoo and set hairdo and perfectly manicured and painted fingernails was no favourite of mine, either. "Does anyone know what le lit might be?" I shot up my hand. Turns out it was nothing to do with the light that I though the word resembled, she was scathing in her ridicule of my genuine response. Oh, so very different from Miss Merrick in primary three – "one of the things I like about Catherine, is that she always puts up her hand and tries her best" – bless that woman and curse Miss Murray. She used to say to the class, when we all took in a sharp breath and let out a squeal, as she accidentally caught her fingernails on the board – "I don't know what you're squealing at, they're my nails" - Catherine soon stopped trying and relished the frequent fingernail incidents.

Miss Murray later redeemed herself by giving me her first floor, double bedroom in the hotel that we took over on a school trip to Belgium; I fell foul of an asthma attack on the first day and sharing with three others on the top floor, bedded and pillowed on feathers did me no favours. Miss Murray did.

School dinners were for kids who qualified for free meals and sissies, never were they considered "cool", not that I ever was! We soon learned where the nearest eateries were. Over the road and round the corner, the bridie and hot apple pie shop, was run by two truly ancient crones. Up the road and round one corner, next to the off-licence, was the hot pie and bean shop, filled rolls were also available there.

I can still feel the sensation of biting into a too hot Scotch pie, topped with baked beans and juggling the lava hot and unstable delicacy in a very soon soggy brown paper bag! I would do that again!! Round the other corner was a café, she served a mug of Heinz soup and stale bread that had been warmed through, to render it soft and edible, I thought the warm bread was a nice touch, Mum was furious when I told her.

We marched up the road to Holy Cross church, to attend Mass and bellow out "exult we in the nude", on the first Friday of every month. Once a week we straggled up and, shivering, back down Calder Street to the local swimming baths and back down again. We survived.

Second year was better, with a new friend of mine, purely because her surname began with "H" and mine with "G", so we were put sitting next to each other, leaving little choice but to become friends. Her parents owned a travel agency at the top of the road, we used to duck in there, escaping from the first Friday Mass march and have an early lunch. In third year, we relocated to the main building in Dixon Avenue, where, among so very many pupils, we were able to gain a level of anonymity and stick with our own wee groups, that suited me just fine.

We crafted misshapen, unidentifiable objects in pottery class; we made unwearable underskirts, in sewing and learned about "hospital corners" in house-wifery. The making of tea and toast, scrambled eggs, apple pie, and jam tarts were among the delicacies in which we were coached. These classes were good fun, the teachers were all nice, perhaps realizing that was the only way to get any results from us!!

We were now at the stage where we had a choice of subjects to study, albeit limited. We were offered careers advice, my advisor was my hated maths teacher, so, you may imagine that went well!!

Lunch time was a step up from Polmadie – the Albert Café was snug and warm to sit in whilst enjoying a roll 'n' sausage, single cigarettes were available to buy, too!!

So, higher education came and went, I escaped with a Higher and a couple of O-Levels, nothing short of remarkable, given that I never did study or revise, I either knew it, or I didn't! I had friends going to University – I could think of nothing worse!! We grew up a bit, too, not so readily shocked or intimidated by our fellow students that hailed from elsewhere. One of whom, was mother to twins at the age of sixteen, the same girl whose Grandmother was the same age as my Mum; they didn't break the circle, perhaps the very kind of circle that Mum was so determined to bypass.

I also survived, as so many did not, the huge gas explosion that devasted Clarkston. I was in Vicky Road, buying new winter boots. Dad and Chris thought I was shopping locally, harnessed up the dog and could only get as close as looking down, from Stamperland Hill, behind Clarkston Hall, on the horrific scene of death and total destruction.

I combed the job vacancy section in the Evening Times and landed the first job that I was interviewed for!! A year later, I had achieved one, spectacularly short-sighted goal of mine, I was earning forty pounds a week. I was better off than better folk, as Mum would say!!

Having arrived for my interview in a torrential downpour and bedraggled as a consequence, I smiled as my future employer introduced himself, saying, – "you do have nice teeth, indeed, dear". Thus, I became a receptionist and surgery assistant for Mr Devine's Dental Practice, in Norfolk Street, just off Gorbals Cross, along at the corner with Eglinton Street.

I loved that job!!! Mum and Dad were right! There was nothing we couldn't do!!

I left Glasgow in 1980, spending a year in Ireland, followed by a year back home. Then, to Mid Wales for fourteen or so years. My partner in this life and I had previously married completely the wrong people, however, we first met in 1994 and have never looked back, celebrating twenty-five years together now!

We have been to Glasgow a great many times in the intervening years, usually to attend a funeral, too many of those, a rock gig where my brother was playing or a BIG birthday party; a couple of experiences stick in my mind. My partner giving an anguished wail from the bathroom – the more he tried to rinse off the shower gel, the more frothy and bubbly it became!!! So used was he to the hard water here, that the perfect, soft waters of Loch Katrine were greatly underestimated and too much shower gel used!!

Upon taking himself along Sauchiehall Street and being caught in a sudden downpour, he was hailed by a passing native of Glasgow – "haw, you've done it!! You've won the wettest shirt of the day!" It just doesn't happen anywhere else!! Only in that Dear Green Place!!

He also delights in buying a pack of chewing gum or something small and paying with a fiver, always necessitating change back.

The shop assistants in Glasgow have their very own version of the American "you're welcome"......... "no/nae problem" or "no/nae bother", this always makes both of us smile. As does overhearing, from the pavement cafes on Royal Exchange Square, a Glaswegian ordering, "cappychino an'a crwassong", the good folks of my home town just do not do pretentious and I love them all the more for it. Mum always said "sangwidge". I once asked Aunt Rose, the sole survivor of Mum's eight siblings, now living in sunny California for the last thirty odd years, what would you say if someone asked why should they visit Glasgow? She answered so readily, "the people", I so readily concur.

It was easy to skip across the shared border with Wales to become happily settled and proud of the "forgotten" county, Shropshire, rural and so like my beloved Ayrshire, yet not really, just me and my Shropshire lad, happy every after.

Mum and Dad really were right, there's nothing that cannot be done.

Jimmy Murphy

A story for Danny Gill as requested

I got this from a lady this Morning here`s how it went..

Jimmy did you work in the Strathy Bingo ......

Yes I did for a couple of Years..

Don`t know if you will remember me.

I used to go to the Bingo with my wee Ma Rachel Faulds many moons ago,

I had my three kids only 11 months apart, you asked my Ma once Is that girl still pregnant, and she said no that`s her having another one.

And you said the First time I see her not pregnant, I will shave my beard off.

The next time i saw you in the orange halls in Mordaunt st many years later.. and lo and behold I was not Pregnant and you had no beard. Remember serving you and you said notice anything. I did not who you were and my Ma said that`s the boy from the Bingo

What a laugh we both had ... hope you are well..

The Beard is back, You pregnant by any chance. lol

Great to hear from you

And the memories are spot on..

I hope you are well And if ye have a boy call him Jimmy lol

Great stuff ye canny make this up

I am sitting here with a smile on my face, and I have you to thank for that....

Cheers

No probs Jimmy, no too old now.

Had 4 girls and 1 boy but sadly he passed away 6 years ago this July. I have 10 Grandkids and 4 Great Grandkids

Great Memories and you have not changed a bit, keep the beard you suit it..

A hope ye don`t mind if a share our wee memory with Glescapals..

Are you on Glecapals.

Not at all pal,.. Yes just started ...

Al put it on Gleascapals the pals will love it.

Thanks to Katyhyde Holmes big cheers Pal.

Authors note: Jimmy Murphy is one of the admins on the "Glesca pals" Facebook site and he kindly sent this wee story to me. Many thanks Jimmy.

Rosmond Syme

My Childhood
I was born in Pollokshaws- - - known as "The Shaws" in the 1950's Rosmond Elizabeth Johnnston.

I started school at Sir John Maxwell's aka "Sir Johns" or "Sir Jakes". My Mum, Dad and older brother Keith moved from Baker street in Shawlands/Langside in 1959/60 to here.

My Dad was a Publican and his pub was the Bay horse on Pollokshaws rd, growing up in Pollokshaws was the best, a great place, we had loads of things to do and places to go and of course we had Sandra's café which became a place that we would gather and meet friends. Many a romance was sealed there too.

I stayed in number 171 Shawbridge street aka "the Holy building" 'well according to my dad, see it was situated between two Churches. Across the road was the "Georgic" building which was once a sort of hotel type Inn. This was frequented by Highwaymen many years ago, from our back green ran a tunnel under Shawbridge street to the "Georgic" building and according to old stories it was used by the Highwaymen.

There was lots of things to do in and around Pollokshaws, there was the Pollok estate as it was referred to then, great picnics were had there and great adventures too. Then there was the Tilly swings park - Auldhouse park, you could play proper tennis there, and putting or just playing about. Shawhill swing park and the two chutes park at Auldhouse rd, the swimming baths and a great library. Oh and Crossmyloof ice-rink which was my second home.

My Mum was from Newcastle but unfortunately died when I was only 7 years old, my Mother was only 42, so a very young woman and my Father was 40 then. So growing up without a Mother was extremely hard for me, how did my Father manage!!

Well it wasn't until I was maybe in my 40's did I realise how hard it must have been for him.

I was sent off to boarding school as my father had a business to run, so he thought it was for the best. I hated it there, it was run by Nun's, some of whom were truly Angels, others were witches in disguise especially my music teacher: who rapped my knuckles with a wooden ruler if I played a key wrong. Cruel at times and not a lot of compassion.

I was miserable there and maybe after 6 years more or less my dad decided it was time for me to come to Pollokshaws with him and my brother. He changed his job and worked around me, changed his lifestyle for me and himself.

When I returned home for good I returned to Sir John Maxwell's school, I was not accepted very well, I spoke very pronounced and politely which caused a lot of bullying and dislike. Other kids thought that I was above them. My dad always said "always remember no one is better than you, and you are no better than anyone else".

These actions greatly upset me, kids can be very cruel and my poor Dad was the person that I blamed, however outside of school I was happy and I packed a lot of various activities into those years.

I was in the Salvation Army singing company for years, also the Brethern, anywhere I could sing in fact. It wasn't because of my beliefs although I was a Christian, I just loved singing and this was my way of doing what I liked best. I also went to the Steamie for my dad on a Saturday morning for which my dad was very grateful for and I loved going there. Sometimes I went with a friend sometimes on my own. Everything washed and dried including hair Lol. As I would be going ice-skating in the afternoon.

Somewhere along the line I got a Saturday job, it was in Saxone's shoe shop in Sauchiehall street in Glasgow town. I gave my Dad the money that I had earned so I did not spend it all at the one time, which was a good idea. I was overdrawn every week and my Dad said that the money I gave him was attached to a piece of elastic ha ha. During those teenage years I did a lot of babysitting, I loved kids and the three that I babysat for were, Jamie, David and Lyndsey and I loved them like my little brothers and sister.

My first job when I left school was as a receptionist with a furniture store in their head office. However the position wasn't available for three months, I thought great no school and a wee holiday before I started working for a living. Oh no said my Dad you're not lying about all day so get a job for those three months, so my friend got me a job in the famous Cohen's factory. Although I was there for three months I think I only worked about two weeks, first of all I ran a needle over my index finger, when that was better I stuck the needle through my thumb and 'am convinced there is still a sliver of that needle in my thumb, so Cohen's was not for me !!.

I also went to college twice weekly for secretarial studies although I had to stop as my Dad had become unwell. I married at 19 in June 1970, our first flat was in Maryhill at Bonawe street at Queens cross. By Christmas of that year I was expecting my first child, my life was becoming happier with each day that passed. My Dad was on cloud 9, overjoyed was an understatement and so looking forward to his first grandchild. Unfortunately my Dad died suddenly on the 31st of July 1971 aged 57, just two weeks before my baby was born. I was devastated but I had to be stronger than I had ever been before in my life as my older brother was in pieces.

My son Douglas John Cairney was born on 14th of August 1971, he was my Fathers double. I fell apart and although I did not realise it at the time I was in awful depression. This was a very difficult time in my life which would manifest in later years. I moved from Maryhill in 1974 to Glasgow's east end, a new estate was built called Greenfield it was in between Shettleson and Carntyne where I made a lot of new friends.

In the next few years I went into nursing, did my hands-on training in the early 1970's, however in the middle of my exams I had to stop as my then husband's work took him away from home. I had no one to look after my son so I had to give up something that I truly loved but my son was more important to me than the job.

In 1977 I had another baby, my daughter Gayle Rosmond Louise Cairney who was born on the 19th of June 1977. I was so thrilled as I was expecting twins, I lost one of them after three months but with the expertise of Dr Robinson and hospital care I had my daughter.

This was a small miracle and because of this, a documentary was made by a TV company called Action Research. My daughters 15 minutes of fame was being seen By pope John Paul the 23rd inside my womb bouncing as if she was on a trampoline, not many people can say that eh!!

So in the late 70's early 80's I did a university course in child psychology and successfully got my degree. My nursing experience did not go completely to waste as I secured a position in a nursing home called Woodhead house out in Kirkintilloch. I held that position for several years till once again my husband's work took him away again. I then had to get work that fitted in with school times. In 1989 we moved to Erskine, I didn't like it at first and took me over a year to settle.

By this time my son was working and my daughter attending her secondary school. I got a job nearer to home and settled down a little more. Then for the next few years my life was good, my son met his future wife and my daughter was studying to be a nursery nurse.

In 1996 it was an extremely horrible year as my husband and I parted. My kids were devastated as I was, my devastation caused my health to suffer, it turned out that I had never really grieved for my Father and paired with my marriage break up caused me to have a health breakdown. It took a long time to come back from that horrible place, my friends and all my family were really worried. With God's help I eventually got stronger and stronger. My daughter had now graduated and specialised in special needs Eg Autism, Asperger's xxxx.

In 2000 the millennium I moved to a new house, this was to become my recovery to better times. My son was married 3 years when my beautiful first grandchild was born Rachael Cairney, I was on cloud 9, two years later my second granddaughter Hannah was born, once again extremely happy.

In 2003 I met a lovely man called John, it had taken me almost 7/8 years to trust or go out with anyone again and I started going out with John. In 2004 my daughter was getting married to David, I was really happy for her but sad too as she was moving on with her life. 2007 my third granddaughter was born, Erin what a joy another little Angel to love. 2009, John and I went on holiday to our favourite place "the Isle of Mull", there are many beautiful places on Mull and we were at "Uisken beach" when John asked me to marry him. I was very surprised as getting married was not in my thoughts although I have to say I was secretly happy. Douglas, Gayle and my family were delighted.

2011 my beautiful grandson Noah was born, a little brother for Erin, not her first choice at that time, a wee sister or a dog would have pleased her more. However by the evening Noah was the best thing since sliced bread, well he did bring a great big fluffy dog with him ha ha. 2014 John and I are getting married after a lot of persuading, I had been extremely hurt in my last marriage and that had left many scars.

We were married in Gleddoch house in March, my daughter Gayle was my maid of honour, granddaughter's Rachel and Hannah were my bridesmaids, my other grandchildren Erin my flower girl and Noah my page boy, Douglas my son gave me away, so you could say it was a "family affair."

August of that year I had some pain in my hand which I could not account for, after several weeks on different painkillers, trips to the doctor and A+E, I got taken into hospital unable to walk as I was in so much pain. After about 3 days of horrendous tests, they finally diagnosed me with acute RH [rheumatoid arthritis]. I was devastated and didn't want to believe it. My Mother had had this affliction RH from the age of 16 which eventually caused her death aged 42.

This illness is an auto-immune disease and therefore makes you vulnerable to infections. I've had this RH for almost 5 years now, life is hard and simple things are so harder to do, but with the help, encouragement and love of my husband John and prayers, I got there.

Douglas is training people to ride motorbikes, my daughter Gayle is now lecturing in child care, my grandchildren, Rachel is 20 now and working, Hannah 17 is still at school. My youngest grandchildren, Erin 12 goes to high school in August and Noah 8 is still at primary school. John and they are my life and that's why life is good.

This is my personal story [account of my life so far].

As you see I have lived in the south, the north, the east and the west of Glasgow but without a doubt, the south side [the Shaws] was the best.

Irene [Donna] Robertson

The suns oot, sun seemed to be oot a lot years ago and hot summer days.. and its the school holidays and the kitchen windaes shoved up and open wide letting the sun stream in hitting the sink where ma mammys whitening ma sannies.. ye mind the wee t strap wans wae the button and hid a wee heel unlike the cheaper wans wae laces... mine were upmarket sannies ye know.. nothing but the best.... then she wid put them oot in a wee neat row, two pairs slanty oan the ledge tae dry... a loved that smell of Properts whitening.. while waitin fur them tae dry she wid brush ma long herr and put it up intae a pony wae wan of they plastic wee clips that hid elastic at the undeside.. must hiv damaged ma herr terrible but a liked it aw tight then she wid tie a big satin bow roon it , ah looked as if a wiz aboot tae take aff... the bow always matched ma dress...nae troosers fur lassies in they days although some days ah wore shorts... Always white ankle soaks completed the look.... then ad jump when wan of ma pals shouted up fur me tae go oot and play.... Gemmes game in and oot of fashion if ye mind... wan week it wid be roller skates where we d steal oor ma s nylons to tie them tight, the metal skates that fitted any size fae a wean to yer da... ye adjusted them in the middle, mine were oot a saleroom in the Gallowgate...American made the good ole USA and a wiz so proud tae tell ma pals that fact.... mind we wid spin the wheels to show aff the ball bearins...they hid wee metal things near the front that ye could tighten roon yer shoes but big elastic bands that yer maw used tae haud up her nylons did the trick tae..but shut aff yer circulation... great times clanking doon the sterrs on oor bums wae oor skates oan.. whit a racket...........other times it wiz peever wae a polish tin usually Kiwi , fulled wae durt tae make it heavier... but a mind ma auntie Margaret brote me a marble wan fae Rothesay and a thote a wiz a toff a real mccoy peever.. then someone knocked it... a wiz devastated ower that for months, even longer............ Ropes were a great pastime in Summer.. even the boys asked furra gemme ... Step the Gallie on we go... aw fur maries wedding.. and I call in my sister..... Cawing the ropes wiz done by taking turns aboot, great exercise no matter if ye were jumpin or no.. Think ma favourite pastime though wiz drawing in the streets wae pipe clye.. mind the stuff ma put in her mop pail tae dae the sterrs, aye that stuff, made great cheap chalk..... hid great time chalking and it also drew the beds for peever........... then some days it wid be doublers. two good stoaters oot the wee paper shoap ower the road.. no tennis baws they were rotten for doublers, it hid tae be good hard rubber stoaters and matching as ye couldnae hiv odd balls for doublers.. it didnae work right... "the old grey mare she aint what she used tae be aint what she used to be..." wae first leg second leg , under, being which wiz jibby.. a think meant Gibralter and twirls.........and one haun.... we wee aw quite proficient at doublers.. .....Kick the can wiz a big time favourite wae aw the weans..then the hula hoop came oot in the late 50s ..got mine fae the Triang shoap at Brigton Cross, loved that big toy shop near Anson street.. best fun ever for ten bob.. and best exercise anaw..... oh tae turn back time....

Chapter 3

Famous Glaswegians

Rikki Fulton

What a performer was our Robert Kerr "Rikki Fulton, born in the Dennistoun district of Glasgow in April 1924 at 46 Appin rd.. When he was three years old the family moved to Riddrie but Rikki returned to Dennistoun for his secondary school education at Whitehill Secondary school.

He started his professional acting career as a straight actor in repertory theatre and BBC radio. He did work down in London for a short while but thankfully he returned to Scotland where he was later to become an acting legend.

Who can ever forget "Francie and Josie" when two street wise Glasgow Teddy boys took the Nation by storm with " Aw Hullawrerrrr China" etc. Yes the "Adventures of Francie and Josie" established Rikki Fulton and Jack Milroy as household names in Scotland starting in 1962.

Rikki still starred in Pantomine " A wish for Jamie " and "A love for Jamie" and straight theatre before later on becoming another instant TV hit with "Scotch and Wry" oh and how we loved the Reverend I. M. Jolly which we still can see on reruns on TV or You Tube. He also had parts in a few films like "Gorky park", "Local Hero", and "Comfort and Joy".

Yes Rikki was a busy man and a much loved star and person.

He performed at the Edinburgh fringe, appeared twice in Rab C Nesbitt and also "Para Handy". Scotch and Wry had a long TV run between 1978 to 1992 becoming a Hogmanay tradition to have us all laughing in hysterics..

Rikki was named Scottish TV personality of the year twice in 1963 and 1979.

He was awarded the Order of the British Empire in 1992 and a year later the lifetime achievement award from BAFTA Scotland.

In 1996 after appearing as "Francie and Josie", for over 36 years Rikki Fulton and Jack Milroy appeared in their "Final Farewell at the Kings Theatre Glasgow. Jack died later in 2001 aged 85.

Fulton's last full performance on TV came on New Years eve 1999 with a comedy special "It's a Jolly Life."

He wrote his autobiography "Is it that time already" was awarded a Doctor of Arts and a Doctor of Letters. In 2002 he was diagnosed with Alzheimers disease, Kate his partner had looked after and cared for him but it got to the stage he had to be moved into a nursing home where he died peacefully in his sleep in January 2004 aged 79 years.

All we can say is thank you so much Rikki Fulton for the years of pleasure you gave to us all and I'm sure you and Jack Milroy will be rehearsing "Francie and Josie" in the clouds above.

Billy Connolly

The Big Yin was born in November 1942 at 69 Dover street Anderston Glasgow, when he was 4 years old he and his older sister Florence moved to Partick to be looked after by two of his Fathers sisters, his aunties Margaret and Mona Connolly.

A life growing up in the old tenements and all that it entailed followed until he started work doing his 5 year apprenticeship as a boilermaker in the shipyards, in 1965 he finished his apprenticeship and after a short while became a folk singer in the Scotia pub in Stockwell st in the Toon.. He formed a folk-pop group duo with his pal Tam Harvey called the "Humblebums", in 1969 they were joined by Gerry Rafferty. Harvey left the trio in 1969 while Connolly and Rafferty made another two albums.

A year previous Billy married Iris Pressagh, they had two kids.

In 1971 the Humblebums broke up, the head of transatlantic records Nat Joseph persuaded Billy to drop the folk singing and become a comedian and as they say the rest is history.

In 1972 Nat produced Connollys first solo album a mixture of comedy songs and short monologues. Come 1974 he sold out the Pavillion theatre, then in 1975 he appeared on the Michael Parkinson TV show and how can we ever forget that "bum" joke which was hilarious and this really took off his national appeal as Parkinsons TV show was shown nationwide and this was the first taste of millions of people to see the Big Yin.

Not long after that he had a couple of hit records with novelty songs "Divorce" and "In the Brownies". In 1979 he met New Zealand born actress Pamela Stephenson on a cameo appearance of "Not the nine o'clock news", he met up with her again in Brighton and told her his marriage was on the rocks. John Cleese and Martin Lewis persuaded Billy to join them in that years "Amnesty" show and he did. He made the film "Water" alongside Michael Caine in 1985, he divorced Iris in

1985. that same year Billy became tee-total his thinking was if Pamela goes away then I am on my own so the choice was easy as he didn't want that.

Connolly completed his first world tour in 1987 so things were definitely looking up for the Big Yin, he married Pamela in Fiji in 1989 and they later had three daughters. He was starting to get big in the USA in the 1990's and appeared in a few good films like "Mrs Brown" and got nominated for a Bafta award.. He then done a world tour of Scotland on his motorbike and done the same in Australia in 1999 and done a 59 date sell out tour of Oz and New Zealand plus a 25 date in London's Apollo theatre in Hammersmith.

More BBC world tours of NZ in 2000 and appeared in the film "The man who sued God" in 2013 he had minor surgery for prostate cancer and was told on the same day he had the early signs of Parkinsons disease. We all wish Billy all the best in his battle against this illness, one of the things I admire about the "Big yin" is he never lost his love for Glasgow. A great career and plenty of laughs over the years he has given us.

Lulu

She was born Marie McDonald McLaughlin Lawrie in Lennox castle in November 1948 and the eldest of four children. She spent her youth growing up in the Dennistoun district of Glasgow in the east end and like most children had a great life growing up in the tenements. She had a flair for singing early on in her life and was always asked to sing at any party's her parents had in their house, some people are born with a bubbly outlook on life and Lulu certainly was /is one of those. In her teenage years she was always singing and sang many weekend nights in the Orange halls roundabout Bridgeton and Dennistoun.

Her first big hit was "Shout " which she sang with her group Lulu and the Luvvers in 1964 and I remember hearing that song being played on all the transistor radios that people seemed to carry about with them in the early part of the swinging 60's and yes I was one of them too.

Then in 1966 she broke with the "Luvvers" and went solo and she had loads of success in singing and TV appearances. In 1967 Lulu made her screen appearance in a hit film called "To Sir with love" about rowdy teenage kids played by some big names of the future Christian Roberts, Judy Geeson, Suzy Kendall etc in the east end of London who are slowly won over by their teacher Sidney Poitier a great film indeed and the icing on the cake was that Lulu sang the title song and had a tremendous hit with it.

In 1968 she become host of her own TV series show "Happening for Lulu" and more TV followed through her life. When she was aged 20, she got married to Bee Gee Maurice Gibb but after 4 years they split up Lulu couldn't put up with his rock and roll lifestyle and excessive drinking.. I think Lulu realised that they were too young to have been married.

In 1977 she married Hairdresser John Frieda and they had a union lasting 20 years with one son being born to them Jordan Frieda. Lulu has stated she had love links with Davy Jones of the Monkeys and David Bowie.

Lulu appeared in a remake of "Guys and Dolls" in one of London's west end theatres, she was also a songwriter and penned the song "I don't want to fight" which was recorded by Tina Turner.

She was awarded an O.B.E. in the year 2000 and also published a book "Lulu's secret to look good" in 2010 and sang in a duet album with Paul McCartney and Elton John.

Now some people like her and others don't but personally I like her but it's down to the individual's choice.

Lulu said in 2010 on the Daily Mail's website "I'm 62 years old this year and people ask you look so good, well I eat well, exercise and know what clothes look good on me."

Jimmy Logan

James Allan Short was born in Dennistoun on 4th of April 1928, he was born into a family of entertainers, he actually took the "Logan" surname from his Aunt" Ella Logan" who was a Broadway performer. Jimmy also has a famous sister called Annie Ross who is and actress and singer. Jimmy was educated at Inverclyde and Bellahouston Acadamy.

He left school at 14 years of age and toured with his family on stage all over Scotland and the North of Ireland. He started off selling theatre programmes then moved onto operating the theatre lights at the age of 8 and performed as a cowboy on stage aged 10, he was assistant manager at 15 and landed his own show at the Metropole theatre in Glasgow aged 19.

His first real acting role was in the film "Floodtide" in 1949, some of his other films were "the wild affair", "Carry on abroad", "Carry on Girls", "Captain Jack", "The debt collector" [with Billy Connolly].

By the mid 1950's Jimmy had appeared at the London Palladium and was earning £500 per week. Jimmy was a very successful Scottish entertainer of his generation. As a young man he had a Rolls Royce, a Private plane, a flat in Culzean castle and a beautiful wife.

Jimmy's rolls Royce number plate was JL 10.

He purchased the Empress theatre for £80.000 in 1964, he refurbished it and reopened it as the new Metropole. He performed a one man musical of the life of Scottish entertainer Sir Harry Lauder which was titled Lauder in 1976. He was awarded an OBE in 1966.

It was when Jimmy was working with that other great actor Stanley Baxter that he made up that famous catch-phrase "Sausages is the boys". Of course Jimmy had bad luck in his life too and when he was only 49 he had no home, no wife , no money, no theatre, no Rolls Royce, no chauffeur, no castle, no plane and no laughs but he bounced back after 3 failed marriages and a quadruple by pass operation, yes Jimmy kept taking the curtain calls.

Jimmy was very happy in his 4th marriage to Angela, and immensely proud of his sister Annie Ross.

He was awarded an honorary doctorate by Glasgow Caledonian university in 1994 and was elected a fellow of the Royal Scottish Academy of music and drama in 1998.

Jimmy also published his autobiography "It's a funny life."

He was very proud of his OBE, he was a generous man of indomitable spirit who bravely faced and fought the cancer that killed him in April 2001.

Yes he was a fine actor and husband/father sadly missed by them all and by the Scottish people.

Alistair MacLean

Alistair Stuart MacLean was born in Glasgow in April 1922, he was the third of four sons he was also a son of a Church of Scotland minister, although born in Glasgow he spent much of his childhood and youth in Daviot which is ten miles south of Inverness. He joined the Royal Navy in 1941, serving in WW2, he spent most of the war as an able bodied seaman and leading torpedo operator. He was discharged in in 1946 and studied English at Glasgow university while also working at the post office and as a street sweeper.

He graduated in 1953 and briefly worked as a hospital porter, then as a teacher at Gallow Flat in Rutherglen. While still a university student MacLean began writing short stories for extra income winning a competition in 1954 with the maritime story "Dileas". The publishing firm Collins asked him for a novel and he responded with "HMS Ulysses" based on his war experience, this was written in three months and sold over a million copies. His next novel "The guns of Navarone" was in 1957 and was about an attack on a fictitious island 400.000 copies sold in the first six months.

The film "the guns of Navarone" in 1961 was very successful at the cinema, he had written "South by Java head", "The last frontier", "Night without end" and "Fear is the key" [1961]. In the early 60's he published 2 novels under the pseudonym "Ian Stuart" in order to prove the popularity of his books was due to content rather than his name, those books were "The dark crusader" and "The Satan bug" [1962] and they both sold well.

He continued writing as MacLean and wrote "The golden rendezvous" and "Ice station zebra" in 1963.

He once said I'm not a novelist, I'm a storyteller. It took him on average 35 days to write a novel. His novels were noted for their lack of sex, he said I like girls I just don't write them well, stating we all know men and women make love - there's no need to show it.

MacLeans books sold so well he moved to Switzerland as a tax exile. While In 63-66 he took a two years break from writing to run a hotel as a business and bought the Jamaica inn on Bodmin moor. During this time a film was made of "The Satan bug" in 1965. MacLean returned to writing in 66 and wrote "When eight bells toll". Producer Elliot Kastner approached MacLean looking for film scripts. Kastner with partner Jerry Gershwin bought five film scripts from MacLean. Then "Where eagles dare" was published in 1967 and the 1968 film was a huge hit. He was writing "Puppet on a chain" and "Caravan to Vaccares" in 1970, these books all began as screenplays for Kastner. Then he wrote "Bear island" in 1971 but most of these latter books didn't turn out to be smash film hits. By 1973 MacLean had sold over 24 million novels!!

He once said I am not a writer I am a business man and writing is my business", he said I read a lot, I travel some but mostly what I don't know then I invent. He also said that he couldn't understand why people bought his novels. He tried his hand with American TV but wasn't too successful with the exception of "The hostage tower" which was approved by CBS and aired in 1980.

MacLeans later works were often worked on by "Ghost writers" with MacLean just producing the basic outline of the book. Then his last novel was "Santorini" [in 1986] but only published after his death.

In his lifetime MacLean constantly struggled with alcoholism and was reported to lock himself away with bottles of whisky and a glass while writing his books. It is reported that this was a factor in causing him to have a stroke in February 1987 which killed him.

He is buried a few yards away from Richard Burton in Celigny Switzerland. He was married twice and had two sons by his first wife as well as an adopted third son.

MacLean was awarded a Doctor of letters by the university of Glasgow in 1985.

Lorraine Kelly

Lorraine was born in Ballater street in the Gorbals district of Glasgow in November 1959.

She is a Scottish TV presenter, journalist and writer. She has presented on TV am, ITV breakfast, Daybreak and Lorraine.

Her family moved from the Gorbals and went to nearby Bridgeton then later onto East Kilbride where she attended Claremont high school. She turned down a university place to study English and Russian in favour of a job on the East Kilbride news [her local newspaper] then joined BBC Scotland as a researcher in 1983. She moved to TV am as an on screen reporter covering Scottish news in 1984. then in 1993 Kelly helped launch GMTV by presenting a range of programmes, she would share the spot with Eamon Holmes.

In 1992 she married Steve Smith a television cameraman and they have one daughter Rosie born in 1994, they live in Berkshire outside of London. Kelly was born of a Catholic mother and a Protestant father.

While living in the Broughty ferry area in Dundee she started supporting Scottish football team Dundee united circa 1987 after being taken there to watch a match by her now husband.

In June 1994 Kelly went on maternity leave but shortly afterwards was sacked form the main presenting roles. Lorraine returned in 1994 to do a mum and baby slot, this led to her becoming presenter at nine o'clock live. The show proved so popular it was moved to an earlier 8.35 am slot retitled Lorraine live.

On September 2010 GMTV ended, with ITV breakfast then taking over, while Lorraine launched alongside Daybreak. In 2011 Kelly presented the ITV series children's hospital, in May 2012 it was confirmed that Kelly would take over from Christine Bleakley on Lorraines sister show Daybreak. While in 2014 Lorraine made a cameo appearance in an episode of "Birds of a feather". She is a celebrity patron of worldwide cancer research and patron of many more worthy causes.

In 2004 she was elected as the first female rector of the university of Dundee, she held this post until 2007.

In June 2008 she was awarded an honorary doctor of laws from the university for her services to charities, in 2012 she was given the OBE in the new years honours list.

In 2014 she received a special Scottish BAFTA award honouring her 30 year television career.

In 2018 she was awarded an honorary degree of doctors of arts from Edinburgh Napier university.

In 2018 Kelly spoke of her experience with the menopause and encouraged others to speak out about it. In 2019 Kelly won a tax case over £1.2 million with the judge deeming that Kelly is a "Self employed star" rather than an employee of TV.

Authors note: I think Lorraine Kelly has done so very well over the years, best of luck to her for the future and all the charities that she helps.

Lonnie Donegan

Born Anthony James Donegan in the Bridgeton district of Glasgow on April 1931 his ethnic mix was Scottish/Irish. He moved at an early age to London with his mother when his parents divorced. He was inspired by blues music and New Orleans jazz bands that he heard on the radio, he resolved to learn the guitar and bought his first one when aged 14.

The first band he ever played in was big trad jazz bands led by Chris Barber who had approached Donegan on a train asking him did he want to join his group.

He also played in Ken Coyles group but this all stopped when he was called up for national service late 1949. After finishing his national service he formed his own group "The Tony Donegan jazzband" and found work around the greater London area.

One night they were the opening band for the main act which was Lonnie Johnson but the MC got the names mixed up and introduced Tony Donegan as Lonnie Donegan by mistake and so the legend of "Lonnie Doegan" was born and as they say the rest is history.

By the mid 1950's a new sound of music appeared on the scene it was called "Skiffle" and Lonnie Doegans skiffle group was a smash hit. In 1955 Donegan had a hit song "Lost John" and it reached number 2 in the UK singles chart.

His success sent him to the USA where he appeared on the Perry Como show and the Paul Winchell show, he returned to the UK in 1956 and made his debut album including "I'm"a rambling man" and "Wabash cannonball", this LP was a big hit securing sales into the hundreds of thousands.

The popular "Skiffle style" encouraged amateurs to get started and one of the many skiffle groups that followed were the "Quarrymen" formed in 1957 by John Lennon.   Donegans "Gambling man/Putting on the style was a UK hit in July 1957 when Lennon first met Paul McCartney.

Donegan went on to sing a series of popular songs like "Cumberland gap" and "Does your chewing gum lose its flavour" [on the bed post overnight] which was his only hit in the USA. He turned to a music hall style with "My old man's a dustman" which was not well received by skiffle fans but never the less it went to number 1 in the UK charts. Lonnie continued to appear regularly in the UK charts before succumbing to the arrival of the Beatles and beat music.

Donegan recorded sporadically through the 1960's including sessions in Nashville Tennessee and in 1964 he became a record producer.

He was "unfashionable" through the 60's and70's and suffered his first heart attack in 1976 in the USA and and had quadruple bypass surgery.

He returned to attention in 1978 when he recorded his earlier songs with Rory Gallagher, Ringo Starr, Elton John and Brian May, the album was called "Putting on the style".By the 1980's he was making regular   concert appearances again.

He then moved from Florida to Spain and in 1992 he had further bypass surgery after having another heart attack. Donegan had a late renaissance in 2000 when he appeared on a Van Morrison album which was held live in Belfast he had previously appeared at the 1998 Glastonbury festival and was made an MBE in 2000.

Paul McCartney said of Lonnie, "He was the first person we had heard of from Britain to get to number 1 in the charts". So we studied his records avidly, we all bought guitars to be in a skiffle group. He was the man.

Lonnie was married a couple of times having two sons Anthony and Peter. Lonnie died in 2002 aged 71.

Robert Carlyle

Robert or Bobby as he likes to be called was born in Maryhill in 1961, the son of Elizabeth a bus company employee and Joseph Carlyle a painter and decorator to trade. He was brought up by his Da after his Ma left when he was four years old. He left school at 16 without any qualifications and working for his Da as a painter and decorator.

However Robert continued his education by attending night classes at Cardonald college in Glasgow. He became involved in drama at the Glasgow arts centre aged 21. He subsequently graduated from the royal Scottish academy of music and drama.

In 1991 he and four friends founded a theatre company "Raindog" which was involved in TV and film work, that same year he guest starred in the "Bill" and also starred in his first movie "Riff-raff" directed by Ken Loach. Then In 1994 he played the gay lover of Father Greg in the film "Priest". Carlyle's first high profile role came as murderer Albert "Albie" Kinsella in an episode of "Cracker" opposite Robbie Coltrane and Christopher Eccleston. This highly acclaimed role showcased Carlyles "pure intensity", after appearing in Cracker he landed the role of Highland policeman Hamish MacBeth, this series ran for three seasons from 1995 - 1997.

In 1996+97 he appeared in the two highest-profiles of his career to date as the psychopathic Francis Begbie in the film "Trainspotting" and also as Gaz the leader of a group of amateur male strippers in the film "The Full Monty". The latter earned Carlyle a BAFTA award for the best actor in a leading role.

He also starred with Ray Winstone in the 1997 film "Face". Carlyle also played Malechy McCourt in the 1999 film adaption of "Angela's ashes" and also played the part of arch villain Renard in the 1999 James Bond film "The world is not enough" and a cannibalistic soldier in the 1999 film "Ravenous".

Robert appeared in the 2002 "Oasis" music video for "Little by little".

He played the part of Adolf Hitler in the 2003 mini series "Hitler, the rise of evil", now in 2006 he played the villain Durza in "Eragon". While in 2007 he played one of the main characters in the film "28 weeks later".

He also played the lead role as a marine engineer attempting to save London from total devastation in the disaster film "Flood", that year he also portrayed Father Joseph Macavoy in the film "Tournament".

In 2008Carlyle narrated a BBC audio-book version of the cutting room. He was cast as Dr Nicholas Rush in the TV series "Stargate universe" in December 2008 Robert appeared in 24: Redemption a TV movie based on the popular 24 starring Keifer Sutherland.

In 2009 Carlyle appeared in a long form commercial for "Johnnie Walker" whisky titled "The man who walked around the world", Carlyle was shown walking down a path and talking for six minutes in a single "long take". the add took two days to film. The director Jamie Rafn afterwards referred to Carlyle as an "Utter genius." He voices the character of Gabriel Belmont and his counterpart Dracula in the video game "Castlevania : Lord of shadows". From 2011 - 2018 Carlyle portrayed Mr Gold [Rumplestillskin] in the fantasy-drama TV series "Once upon a time", the character is a Wizard, deal-maker and manipulator.

Known for his commitment to authenticity in acting roles Carlyle has often changed his life style and physical appearance to gain a better understanding of the character he is to play and is noted for removing two of his own teeth before reappraising his role as Begbie in "T 2 Trainspotting".

He has been married to make up artist Anastasia since 1997 and have three children.

Authors note: Well done to Robert [Bobby] and all the other famous Glaswegians mentioned by me above for the pleasure that you have given to us over the years and for being the Patron of the Benny Lynch statue campaign.

Chapter 4

Bits and pieces

The Shell monument

This 15 inch howitzer shell was made by William Beardmore + Co. and was converted into a charity collection box after the first world war. It stood for many years in the middle of the station concourse and was a favourite meeting place for courting couples.

The shell was removed from the centre of the concourse in 1966 and now stands forlornly in a corner near to the Gordon street entrance to the station,

There was also a shell monument [smaller one] that once stood in St Enochs old railway station but its the one in the central that is remembered most by people.

The Song/the Memory

How many of us over the years when on hearing a song being played can identify it with an event or something that has happened to us earlier in our lives? My memory of that "certain song" is when I lived and worked back in Australia in the mid 1970's. I was working outside of Sydney city in the "sticks" [meaning far away from the urban area] but not far enough to call it "the bush".

Anyway we started building bricks at 6 am and finished work at 2.30 in the afternoon because at finishing time it could be so hot some days you could burn your hand picking up your "bead" [metal spirit level]. One of the other bricklayers John, lived beside me in Sydney city and used to drive me to work and back.

This day after we had finished work we were driving over Sydney Harbour bridge in his "mini-moke" which was like a small land rover but with completely no cover over it. He said to me watch my foot on the accelerator, he never put any more pressure on it but as we reached then passed the middle of the Harbour bridge we started to "speed up" as there is a 14 feet camber over the bridge span.

Just as this was happening a song from his car radio started to play "Rock your Baby" by George McCrae as I was drinking an ice cold can of coca-cola which I had just bought from the "gas station" when John had stopped 5 minutes previously to fill up his petrol tank.

The sun was baking hot and there was me about eleven thousand miles from Glasgow, drinking a coke, travelling over the iconic Sydney Harbour bridge, being paid $50 per shift which was great money back in 1974, yes just sitting there wearing a T-shirt, shorts and a pair of trainers 26 years old and listening to "Rock your Baby".

That is why every time I hear that song being played I think of the Sydney Harbour bridge when I was a young man.

That Subway smell

Can you remember years ago when you walked down the tunnel onto the Glasgow subway platforms you caught a "whiff" of that subway smell, well its never left me. I am only back to Glasgow once a year on holiday as I now live in sheltered housing in the borough of Lewisham in south London but I remember that "subway smell" still.

I have travelled on Glasgow's subway a few times in the last few years but I can only catch a tiny wee "whiff" of what it used to smell like, I suppose with better ventilation this has taken the "whiff" away or lessened it but I'm sure that people of my age will agree with me that it was there all those years ago and it is always one of my abiding memories of the Glasgow of old.

Pub hours

I remember as a young man living in Glasgow that the pubs opened from 11 am till 2.30 pm and 5 pm till 10 pm, of course I only had money at the weekends with getting paid on a Friday night. In those far off days there was smoking in all the pubs and usually the only food you got was Scotch pie and peas/beans this was way back in the mid to late 1960's before I left Glasgow on my travels as a bricklayer.

As soon as it reached closing time, the barmen would start screaming out, time please, drink up, c'mon the Polis will be here in a minute !!. this was really annoying especially on a Friday or Saturday night when you still had money in your pocket and it was only 10 pm.

Of course what we had done beforehand [on many an occasion] was to have got a "carry out" from the off sales department of the pub to go to somebody's house for a sing song and if the people of the house you went to never had a record player it was then "spin the bottle" time to see who started the singing first.

Come a Sunday back in those days it was murder Polis if you wanted a drink, the pubs were all closed and you would have to look for a Hotel that held a 7 day drinking license and believe me these Hotels were packed to the rafters with punters wanting a drink on a Sunday. Of course a lot of times on a Sunday you were skint till next pay day !!

It's crazy now when you look back on those days because nowadays we have pubs that serve drink from 9 am [only a few] providing you eat something. Then most of the other pubs open from 11 am right through non stop till 12 pm and you can drink in an easy going atmosphere, well up to about 8 pm in the city pubs, Then you have other bars that have an early morning licence till the early hours of the morning, so if you were out at 8 am you could drink till the wee small hours. [if you can last]

The Glasgow that I left behind in 1968 and the pub hours have changed so much since then but thankfully Glaswegians are still the happy go lucky people that were about in my youth. Could you imagine what people would say today if they said pubs will be closed on Sundays ?. World War III would break out lol.

Co-op Divvy number

How many of us still remember our Ma's divvy number at the co-operative shop?. Well it was drilled into us all when we were weans and I still remember my Ma's – 57824. The last thing your Ma shouted to you as you were going down the tenement stair to the Co-op was "And don't forget mah number". Our Ma's got a dividend twice a year [or was it once] and she would get some money back as a rebate.

With this money she would buy some clothes and a few other things that were on her list and us weans always got a few penny's to buy sweeties didn't we?.

I still remember the Co-op shop my Ma used it was on Rutherglen Rd/Snowdon street in the Hutchesontown area of the Gorbals. I stood there next to Ma as a 5 year old boy mesmerised as the cashier took Ma's money, placed it in a wee cup that was attached to an overhead wire and it zipped its way up to the main cashier sitting at her place high above us.

She took the money and put the change back into that wee cup and it zipped its way on the overhead wire back down to us. To me through my weans eyes it was like something out of "Flash Gordon".

Oh and I just remembered there was always sawdust spread all over the floor, yes the Co-operative shops were very popular with Glaswegians with that dividend payout.How many of you reading this can remember your Ma or Granny's divvy number ??

The Hula Hoop craze

In Glasgow in the late 1950's early 60's we had a craze that took us over with a passion. It was a big plastic ring which was very light in weight and you stood in the middle of it and you would sway your hips like a Hula Hula dancer. You had to try and keep the Hula Hoop sliding up your body. It seemed the faster you went the better chance you had of it stopping from falling down to your ankles.

It sure did make you feel fit [or exhausted] but your head would be spinning sometimes. Then as soon as this craze started it seemed to finish, if I remember correctly it lasted for a few months in the summer time but what a craze.

The Barras

The Barras market has a long tradition in the east end of Glasgow, with hawkers selling from hand carts in the early part of the 20-th century. Of course the barras became more "updated" with the building of the McIvers sheds and the Barrowland ballroom.

The present ballroom was rebuilt in 1960 after a fire in 1958.

Who can remember walking along the Gallowgate or London rd on a Sunday and before you got there you could feel the buzz of the barras, I remember as a wean walking over there one Sunday and one of the side shows was "Paddy the strongman" and he would tear up telephone directory's with his bare hands.

Then I saw him being padlocked by his assistant and a sack placed over his head and his assistant was shouting out that the world record held by Houdini is fifteen minutes to get free of these padlocks and take the sack off of his head. I clearly remember watching this and Paddy was only a minute into his act when a shout went up "Its the Polis" well the world record by Houdini was broken in one minute flat. With him running away down one of the side streets.

His assistant would have walked round the crowd with a "bunnet" for onlookers to chuck a few coins in but if caught they could be arrested. Then you had the man with the wee monkeys and you could get your photo taken with the monkeys on your shoulder and not forgetting the Indian snake oil man.

Listening to the patter of the salesmen at the barras selling their wares was really out of this world and the place would be absolutely packed this was in the 1950's + 60's when I used to walk over there from the soo-side.

There was always plenty of wee cafes to have something to eat or the hot chestnut man in winter time. As I became a teenager I loved looking at the record stall with cheap single records and LP's,

So many different characters used to be about the barras back in those days but now I believe its only a shadow of what it used to be like and there has been talk of clearing the area and building flats there.

People used to come from near and far to the barras and in fact some folk from out-laying districts down in Ayr etc used to hire coaches to take fifty people or so there for the day, Christmas time was special at the barras too with plenty of Christmas time bargains.

The Sub crawl

Being away from Glasgow for so many years I never realised there was such a thing as a "Sub Crawl", I happened to be standing in the Laurieston bar in Bridge street in the Gorbals having a drink in the lounge bar with friends that I hadn't seen in many a year [but met up through face-book] any way it was a Saturday afternoon and there was my company about eight people sitting cosy enough round our table and only a handful of other customers.

All of a sudden the Lounge door opened and within five minutes the lounge was absolutely packed to the rafters, there had to be at least 50 to 60 people and they had one or two quick drinks but within 25 minutes they had all gone !!

I was dumbfounded !! until I was told that people join this "Sub Crawl" do it for a charity of their choice, they meet up and visit every pub nearest to every subway station.

They have one or two drinks in the pub, [alcoholic or not] then get back onto the subway train and get to the next pub and have another drink until they have completed the 15 pubs nearest to the 15 subway stations.

Then after they had all left all the barmen came out cleaned all the glasses from the tables. Made the pub clean again and within twenty minutes another 50 or 60 people had came into the Laurieston bar and the procedure happened all over again. I think that people who partake in the sub crawl say they will give a certain amount of money to charity if they complete all the pubs or just give a donation.

I think its a good cause as long as you can hold your drink but what a shock I got when this happened to me, of course all the pubs on the "Subway Crawl" do a roaring trade Eh.

Old TV shows

I remember my Ma and Da getting a wee black and white TV set in the mid 1950's and we were the only ones to have one in our tenement street, all our neighbours used to come and chap on our door just to look and see what this "new invention looked like". It didn't have to be turned on they just wanted to see what it looked like.!!

We had TV shows like Sergeant Bilko on a Friday night and how we loved all the capers he got up to, remember this was TV in its infancy for us because we used to always go the Picture hoose for entertainment back in those days. We had Dale Robertson acting the part of Jim Hardy in "Wells Fargo" a cowboy adventure, then we had "Quatermass" a science fiction thriller that was on Saturday nights.

Then we only had the one TV channel, BBC 1 but in the late 1950's we got another channel called ITV [with advertisements] and they gave to us in 1960 our first "soap" it was called Coronation street with

Elsie Tanner, Ena Sharples, Albert Tatlock etc the nation was well and truly hooked.

Then we had the One o'clock gang show with Larry Marshall, Dorothy Paul, Jimmy Nairn, Charlie Sim and Moira Broadie it was a brilliant show dealing with news topics of the day and the gang giving us all a laugh with funny acts, it only seems like yesterday eh !!

Then you had shows like Emergency ward 10 and who can ever forget Bonanza with Ben Cartwright, his sons Little Joe, Hoss and Adam all living on the Ponderosa ranch. Then another soap called Crossroads and I could name so many more. Of course the highlight of the year was Hogmanay and Andy Stewart etc welcomed in the Bells but the TV closed down airing just after 11 pm although the Hogmanay show was allowed to continue till 12.30. am.

I loved those old black and white TV shows as I'm sure many of you reading my book will remember them too. Of course nowadays we have television on 24/7 and hundreds of TV channels to choose from but I look back with great fondness to those early days of TV.

Benny Lynch

Benny Lynch was Scotland's first world champion by the age of 22 but his career was over when he was 25 and he was dead by 33.

No wonder the meteoric rise and fall of the boxing legend often referred to as the people's champion still generates interest 70 years after his death.

The latest telling of the story of the diminutive tough guy from Glasgow's Gorbals is a new documentary, Benny, to be screened at the Glasgow Film Festival.

Born in 1913, Lynch rose from being a sickly child in the poverty-stricken tenements to become world flyweight champion.

But his descent was as steep as his rise and just over a decade later he was dead, following a battle with malnutrition and alcoholism.

Seamus MacTaggart, one of the producers of the film, says he wanted to focus on Lynch's achievements as a boxer and not his tragic decline.

He says: "When you see the fantastic archive we have it really gives you sense of how hard he could hit".

"These guys were way under eight and a half stone (54kg) but you look at the ferocity of the punches and also the speed at which they moved and it is amazing".

"He could punch with both hands and hit as hard with each of them. When he was at his prime, no-one could touch him."

Lynch managed 119 fights in his short career.

He won the world flyweight title in 1935 when he beat Jackie Brown in Manchester, reportedly flooring his opponent eight times before the bout was stopped in the second round.

Jim Watt, who became lightweight world champion 40 years later in 1979 said Benny was the first one to win a boxing world championship, he was the forerunner of all the Scottish World Champions who would later follow in his footsteps.

Authors note: I am proud to say that others including myself have been active in trying to get the funds together to erect a statue erected to Benny Lynch's boxing feats over the last few years.

We are well over the halfway line [or more] in getting the funds, its all done voluntarily, we hold fund-raisers, get online donations and try and keep the campaign as much in the public eye as we can with lots of events.

Glasgow Cross

The seven storey Tolbooth steeple is Glasgow cross's most important feature and it is topped by a clock and a stone crown. This was once part of a much larger building, the Tolbooth, which provided accommodation for the Town Clerk's office, the council hall and the city prison.

The debtors prison had a steady stream of inmates who "elected" their own "Provost" and generally ran the place like an exclusive club. They produced their own regulations, including one from 1789 which stated "it is firmly and irrevocably agreed upon that the members of these rooms shall not permit the jailor to turnkey's to force any person or persons into their apartments, who are thought unworthy of being admitted. There was even a rule about celebrating freedom: "Every member, when liberated, shall treat his fellow-prisoners with one shillings worth of what liquor they think proper".

The Tolbooth provided the backdrop to many of the city's dramas and it was here that witches, thieves and murderers were summarily dealt with, by hanging if necessary. It also had a special platform from which the proclamations were read, important in the days before general literacy. The paved area [the plainstanes] in front of the Tollbooth was the "in place" to be seen and here the rich paraded in their finery, particularly the Tobacco Lords, attired in red cloaks and sporting gold-topped canes.

Glasgow cross developed as a communication hub with stagecoaches from Edinburgh and London bringing visitors and news and a reading room in the Tolbooth providing newspapers.

However as the city expanded and moved westwards, the Tolbooth was abandoned and eventually demolished leaving the steeple as an isolated reminder of bygone days. This tragic loss of an important building was the result of the work of the city improvement trust which had the unenviable task of ridding the city of its slums.

Glasgow Central

Deep in the bowels of Glasgow Central Station is a forgotten world in which skilled Victorian engineers and an army of hard-working Glaswegians, displaced Highlanders and refugees from the Irish potato famine strove mightily to lay the foundations of the majestic structure we have today.

A fascinating insight into the birth of the railways in Glasgow is provided by superb guided tours which take the visitor down into the depths, three levels below the busy concourse.

And it has to be said that the main reason for the success of the tour project is down to the guide - Paul Lyons, whose mix of mischievous humour, a few touches of drama and an immense knowledge of the station's history brings the whole thing to life in a fascinating way.

The tours have emerged from Paul's personal odyssey to discover more about life underneath the station - he has spent hour after hour exploring musty old passageways, long deserted platforms and cavernous storage cellars in order to develop the story.

Wearing high visibility jackets and hard hats, 18 of us joined Paul on the main concourse, before slipping through a fairly insignificant doorway into a sort of Alice Through the Looking Glass experience. Paul's commentary concentrates much on social history, the sort of conditions workers experienced in the building and operation of the station.

Perhaps the most poignant moment emerged when Paul described the scenes when the bodies of soldiers, brought home from the Somme during the First World War, were stored in the station, awaiting identification by grieving relatives.

Paul has plans to develop a museum and it is hoped a spur line can be opened, enabling a steam engine to once more pull alongside the

Victorian platform. More and more people are beginning to take notice of the tours and I think it might be a good idea for senior schools in Glasgow to consider allowing pupils to experience them - a brilliant history lesson in the making.

In the Summertime

Do you remember those hot summers we used to know when we were weans growing up. It used to get that hot it melted the tarmacadam on the pavements and we got that thirsty we used to beg oor Ma's to buy us a Jubbly or was it a Jubilee ?[triangular shaped frozen orange lolly] and how it froze your hands it was that cold.

Your Ma used to whitewash your sannies and leave them on the windae sill to dry in the hot sunshine, when they were dry you put them on to go down the stair to play with your wee pals in the street but your Ma's last words to you were don't you dare get any "taur" on them.

It was time to play a game of "rounders" with your pals [a game the USA copied off of us and called it baseball.

Then you would be playing all day in the sunshine and if you got hungry while playing you would always shout up to your Ma's windae "aw Ma gonny threw me doon a piece on jam", of course your Ma always obliged and when she threw it out the windae wrapped in bread paper it would land with a splat at your feet and you had it devoured in thirty seconds flat because you wanted to quickly get back to the game you were playing with your pals.

Here's a wee question for you all, with that many weans living in the tenements how come your Ma knew it was your voice when you shouted up for a piece, but she did didn't she?

Chapter 5

Glasgow Football Clubs

Glasgow football clubs
in alphabetical order

The Celtic Football Club

Celtic (Sel-tik) is a professional football club based in Glasgow, Scotland, which plays in the Scottish Premiership. The club was founded in 1887 with the purpose of alleviating poverty in the immigrant Irish population in the East end of Glasgow. They played their first match in May 1888, a friendly match against Rangers which Celtic won 5–2. Celtic established themselves within Scottish football, winning six successive league titles during the first decade of the 20th century. The club enjoyed their greatest successes during the 1960s and 70s under Jock Stein when they won nine consecutive league titles and the 1967 European cup.

Celtic have won the Scottish league championship 49 times, most recently in 2017-18, which was their seventh consecutive championship. They have won the Scottish cup 38 times and the Scottish league cup 18 times. The club's greatest season was 1966–67, when Celtic became the first British team to win the European cup, also winning the Scottish league championship, the Scottish cup, the League cup and the Glasgow cup. Celtic also reached the 1970 European cup final and the EUFA cup final, losing in both.

Celtic have a long-standing fierce rivalry with Rangers, and the clubs are known as the Old Firm, seen by some as the world's biggest football derby. The club's fan-base was estimated in 2003 as being around nine million worldwide, and there are more than 160 Celtic supporter's clubs in over 20 countries.

An estimated 80,000 fans travelled to Seville for the 2003 UEFA Cup Final.

Clyde FC
Not to be confused with Clydesdale FC or Clydebank FC.

Clyde Football Club are a Scottish semi-professional football club based in Cumbernauld, who play in Scottish league two. Formed in 1877 at the River Clyde, the team play their home games at Broadwood stadium.

The Clyde Football Club was founded and played on the banks of the River Clyde at Barrowfield. Documentary evidence from the SFA and indeed match reports in the Glasgow press clearly show it all began in 1877, and the thread continues unbroken to this day.

Here's how the SFA recorded Clyde's origins:
"Clyde:- Founded 1877; Membership 50; Grounds (private), Barrowfield park, on the banks of the Clyde; ten minutes walk from Bridgeton Cross; Club House on grounds; Colours, White & Blue. Hon. Secretary, John D. Graham, 24 Monteith Row." No longer classed as a Glasgow side now.

Partick Thistle F.C.

Partick Thistle Football Club (nicknamed the **Jags**) are a professional football club from Glasgow, Scotland.

Despite their name, the club are based at Firhill stadium in the Maryhill area of the city, and have not played in Partick since 1908.

The club have been members of the Scottish football league (SPFL) since its formation in 2013. Thistle currently compete in the Scottish Championship, the second tier of the SPFL structure, following relegation via play-offs from the Scottish Premiership in the 2017–18 season.

Since 1936, Thistle have played in their distinctive red-and-yellow jerseys of varying designs, with hoops, stripes and predominantly yellow tops with red trims having been used, although in 2009 a centenary kit was launched in the original navy-blue style to commemorate 100 years at Firhill.

Since 1908 the club have won the Scottish second division once and the Scottish first division (second tier, now the Scottish championship) six times, most recently in 2013. Thistle have won the Scottish cup and the Scottish league cup in 1921 and 1971 respectively.

The club are currently managed by Gary Caldwell, following the departure of Alan Archibald. Under Archibald's management, the club achieved promotion to the newly formed Scottish Premiership in 2013, and remained there for five consecutive seasons.

During this spell Thistle secured major investment and in 2017 finished in the top six of Scottish football for the first time in over three decades.

Key players such as club legend Kris Doolan broke numerous records and became one of the club's top goal scorers.

Despite relegation in the 2017-18 season, Archibald remained as Thistle's manager. However, after a Poor start to the 2018-19 Scottish Championship campaign, Archibald's 5 year tenure came to an end.

Queens park FC

Queen's Park F.C.
Not to be confused with the New Zealand football club Queens park AFC, the English football club Queens park Rangers. or the Welsh football club Gap Queens park FC..

Queen's Park Football Club is a Scottish football club based in Glasgow. The club is currently the only fully amateur club in the Scottish professional Fotball league; its amateur status is reflected by its Latin motto 'Ludere Causa Ludendi' – 'To Play for the Sake of Playing'.

Queen's Park is the oldest association football club in Scotland, having been founded in 1867, and is the oldest outside England and Wales. Queen's Park is also the only Scottish football club to have played in the F A Cup final, achieving this feat in both 1884 and 1885.

The club's home is a Category 4 stadium; the all-seated Hampden park in South East Glasgow, which is also the home of the Scottish national team.

With 10 titles, Queen's Park has won the Scottish cup the third most times of any club, behind Rangers and Celtic although their last such win was in 1893.

Rangers F.C.

Rangers Football Club are a football club in Glasgow, Scotland, who play in the Scottish premiership, the first tier of the Scottish professional football league. Their home ground, Ibrox stadium, is in the south-west of the city in the Govan district. Although not part of the official name, the club is occasionally referred to as **Glasgow Rangers**.

Rangers have won more league titles and trebles than any other club in the world, winning the league title 54 times, the Scottish cup 33 times and the Scottish league cup 27 times, and achieving the treble of all three in the same season seven times. Rangers won the European cup Winners cup in 1972 after being losing finalists twice, in 1961 (the first British club to reach a EUFA tournament final) and 1967. A third runners-up finish in Europe came in the EUFA cup in 2008. Rangers have a long-standing rivalry with Celtic, the two Glasgow clubs being collectively known as the Old firm, which is considered one of the world's biggest football derbies.

Founded in February 1872, Rangers were one of the 11 original members of the Scottish football league and remained in the top division continuously until the Liquidation of The Rangers Football Club PLC at the end of the 2011-12 season. With a new corporate identity the club gained admittance to the fourth tier of Scottish league football in time for the start of the following season. Rangers secured promotion and today are back playing in the Scottish premier league under the guidance of their manager Steven Gerrard.

Third Lanark FC

Third Lanark Athletic Club were a professional Scottish football club based in Glasgow. Founded in 1872 as an offshoot of the 3rd Lanarkshire Rifle Volunteers, they were founder members of the Scottish football association (SFA) in 1872 and the Scottish football league (SFL) in 1890. They played in the top division of the SFL for the majority of their existence, and were League champions in 1903-04. They also won the Scottish cup twice, in1889 and 1905. Third Lanark went out of business in 1967 as a result of mismanagement, six years after having finished in third place in the SFL. Their former ground, Cathkin park in Crosshill, is still partially standing and used for minor football.

In 1996, an amateur football club also called "Third Lanark" was founded with intentions of restoring the club name to senior football and returning to play regularly at Cathkin Park.

Chapter 6

Topics

Lewis's

This the finest of buildings in Glasgow's Argyle st was formerly owned by Mr John Anderson and it was commonly known as Anderson's Polytechnic or just "The Poly", after he sold it to Lewis's in 1929 most people then called it Lewis's Polytechnic or just the "Poly" then as the years went by it became mainly known as just Lewis's.

Do you remember walking along Argyle st and taking a step inside this wonderful store.

I remember when I was about 5 years old and my Ma took me into Lewis's and this was the first time in my life that I had saw "the moving stairs" to us weans it was magic going up and down the escalators, just standing still and the stairs moved you along was magic.

There was so much to see on the different floors but obviously us weans loved the toy department , even if our Ma's never had enough money to buy us anything it was just magic to look at all the different toys. Not forgetting you had an open restaurant upstairs and later on [when I was a young man] a cafeteria on the basement floor.

Christmas time was something special at Lewis's as I'm sure you will remember providing your my age or thereabouts. All the windows were covered in those flashing fairy lights and model Elf's and Gnomes on show too. Of course the icing on the cake if you were a wean was queueing up for a visit to Santa's grotto, only drawback was you had to queue up for a couple of hours at the back stairs , patiently waiting on your turn to come and sit on Santa's knee and he would reach into his sack and give you a present [of course your Ma or Da had paid for the privilege of us to see Santa that's why we got a wee present].

When I started work way back in 1963 I would go with my pocket-money and go to the music department down in the basement and you would cram into one of the "music booths" and listen to the record that you wanted to buy, if you were with your pals then three of you would cram into this booth and listen to the record of your choice. I clearly remember back in 1964 that a single 45 rpm disc cost 6/8d in old money and that meant for one old pound note you could buy three single records or better still for 30 shillings in old money you could buy an LP Of course there was such a great selection of different foods on sale and clothes to buy, it really was such a wonderful store. I'm sure we all have great memories of going to Lewis's but sadly it closed in the 1990's, on my visits back to Glasgow [once a year from London] I stand and look at what used to be Lewis's store and it saddens me it's not there any more, of course the building is still there but with Debenhams taking a good part of it and a few other smaller store names it's just not the same any more but oh what wonderful memories.

The Pawn Shop

Without the Pawn shop years ago lots of people would have went hungry . It was a God send to mothers who sometimes were at their wits end to make ends meet and many a time on a Monday morning the man of the house had his best suit pawned to get money to feed the family through the week.

I remember going with my wee granny Hendry to the pawn shop in Braehead st [Oatlands/Gorbals] it was called John McIntyre's, I remember walking up the stairs and my granny and me would slide into the wee cubicle and she would pass over to the assistant whatever she wanted to pawn that day.

The assistant always asked for your name so it could be put it onto the Pawn ticket and granny would always say it in a whispered voice in case the person in the next cubicle would hear you and recognise you [oh the shame].

Of course come a Friday night and the man of the house gave his wife the wages, she would be round to the Pawn shop in a flash to redeem her husbands suit that she had only pawned on the Monday. Come Monday morning and the whole rigmarole would start all over again, yes the Pawn shop helped many a poor soul out back in those far off days

Bridge street Railway Terminus

Lots of people today take for granted that the Central station has always been the "end of the line" for trains but they would be wrong because before the Central station was built all trains terminated at Bridge street terminus in the Gorbals [no not the subway station]. Bridge street main line station line terminal was built between 1839-41 and opened in 1841, then the railway line was extended over the river Clyde to become what we know today as Glasgow Central station. The Central station opened in 1879, between 1901-1905 the Central station was refurbished and extended over Argyle street with 13 platforms being built.

Hogmanay

Oh how I loved seeing in the new year years ago, I clearly remember my Ma would have the hoose in the old tenement cleaned spotless. All of us weans were scrubbed clean and put to bed but at 11 am we were roused out of our beds to see in the new year alongside our parents and all the first footers who would come to visit us and wish everybody a happy new year.

My Ma and Da had a wee black and white TV set in the mid-1950's and we would sit there looking at Andy Stewart bringing in the Ne'erday, the countdown was on and it was 10, 9, 8 etc and then the bells chimed and the boats on the river Clyde would be blowing their horns [we lived beside the Clyde]. Our tenement house door was left ajar and soon we had our first footers coming in with a lump of coal for good luck and Ma and Da always had whisky, rum and beer on the kitchen table with enough Dundee cake and currant bun and mince pies to feed a battalion.

My sister and me would be sitting either under the kitchen table or hiding behind the sink windae curtain drinking cordial wine and shortbread while listening to everyone taking their turn to sing a song. Of course back in those days the TV ended by 11 pm usually but because it was the bells the TV finished at half an hour past midnight, just as Andy Stewart was getting into the swing of things lol.

I always remember saying to myself when I was about 8 or 9 years old, oh I wish I was grown up so I could drink whisky and sing a song, well my wish came true when I turned 18 and I never needed any persuasion to sing a song at the bells.

Those days in the auld tenements were the happiest days of my life, everyone knew each other, we all helped each and other whenever we could, our Ma's would never miss their turn of the stairs and you played with all your wee pals in the streets while under the watchful eyes of the neighbours who were doing their windae- hingin duty. As I grew up into a young man I had a few Ne'erdays back in Glasgow but I left Glasgow when I was 20 years old and it just wasn't the same celebrating the bells in other countries. I live here in south London in sheltered housing and no one celebrates the Ne'erday but I always sit watching the countdown to the bells on the TV and I raise my glass of whisky to the memory of my loved ones no longer with me and my toast is always a happy new year to all my own family and friends but at the same time my mind flits back to the old tenement days when we were all one.

The Cuban Missile Crisis

In 1962 when I was a 14 year old schoolboy the world was on the edge of World war III, the USA under President Kennedys administration had discovered that nearby Cuba had nuclear warhead heads sited all over their country and it would only be a short period of time if the missiles were launched before they landed in city's of the States.

The whole World held its breath as Russia sent a fleet of ships heading for Cuba. Then the US established a naval blockade to prevent further missiles being delivered to Cuba.

This was all that people in the street were talking about and I clearly remembering going to my secondary school Holyrood and asking the teacher a Mr Keaney what did he think and he said looks like we are all going to die!!! Oh I thought I'm only 14 and won't see my 15th birthday!!

Then after tense negotiations an agreement was reached between President John F Kennedy and Nikita Krushchev, the Soviets would dismantle their offensive weapons and return them to the Soviet union subject to united nations verification in exchange for a US public declaration and agreement not to invade Cuba again. Secretly the US agreed it would dismantle all US built missiles which had been deployed in Turkey aimed at the Soviet union.

So after the 13 day stand off between October the $16^{th} - 28^{th}$ 1962 the World could breathe easy again but what a worrying time for us all who were around at the time.

Both the US President Kennedy and Chairman Krushchev had to be applauded for bringing us back from the abyss's of what could have been WW3, you had to have personally lived through the Cuban missile crisis to have experienced the fear that we all went through and yes I was glad that I could see my 15 th birthday [and more as I'm 71 now as I write.] I just hope that in the future, Leaders of Countries who find themselves in situations that can lead to war have the same foresight as President Kennedy and Chairman Krushchev showed at that time of the Cuban missile crisis.

Celtic v Rangers
Rangers v Celtic

We all know that there is a Green/Blue or Blue/Green divide in Glasgow, that is the way it has always been and will continue to be so for the foreseeable future. There's no good trying to hide it or sweep it under the carpet as if it doesn't exist. Of course it gives both set of fans great pleasure to win the "old firm match" and the atmosphere is absolutely "electric" when the match is being played and both sets of players play the match in a robust and sometimes passionate style and the lead up to the old firm match is always bubbling with anticipation.

When the match is over either the Blue or Green side of Glasgow celebrates while the other can only say "just wait till the next match". This match is watched all over the world as there are many Glaswegian ex-pats living in countries all over the world and this passion for the team that you support is not for the faint-hearted.

Although I remember years ago the Paddy Crerand of Celtic and Jim Baxter of Rangers were great pals on and off the pitch.

Paddy Crerand and Jim Baxter,
adversaries on the pitch, pals off of it.

I remember at one old firm match that Willie Henderson of Rangers fouled Jimmy Johnstone of Celtic, not a bad foul just physical contact as happens when you are playing with passion. Anyway Jimmy gets

92

up and starts wagging his finger at Willie while both sets of fans were screaming murder polis but it transpired that Jimmy was saying to Willie "hey if you foul me again I'm not buying you a pint tonight" as they were meeting up later that night for a drink but the fans thought there was a war of words going on between the two players. One thing I could never understand was that if your team in the old firm match was getting well beaten some supporters would be leaving the ground in droves. It's your team and you should support them win, lose or draw.

Tragedy sometimes can strike at football matches and I will mention two of them, in 1957 Clyde were playing Celtic at Shawfield Stadium on the 14th of December, there was a good crowd there that Saturday and was normal lots of young boys would be sitting in front of the boundary wall that separated the crowd from the pitch.

Well this day a terrible event happened Billy McPhail scored a goal to put Celtic in front and as the crowd surged forwards to celebrate a 50 yard section of the boundary wall collapsed and fell over on the young fans sitting on the grass in front of it.

All the players from both teams rushed over and with the crowd tried to lift the wall off of the injured people underneath it. Sadly a young Celtic fan James Ryan aged 12 died of his injuries, altogether 24 boys and 12 adults were injured and taken to hospital.

Then in 1971 we had the Ibrox disaster which was a crush among the crowd at an old firm match which led to the deaths of 66 people and 200 injured. It happened on 2nd of January 1971 at stairway 13 at Ibrox park [now Ibrox stadium]. It was the worst British football disaster until the Hillsborough disaster in 1989. The match was attended by 80.000. fans and in the 90th minute Jimmy Johnstone put Celtic ahead 1-0 then just a minute later Colin Stein equalised for Rangers. Some say that the fans who had been leaving down the stairway had rushed back up to celebrate and someone fell and the crowd just snowballed causing the deaths but this was indicated not to be true at the official enquiry.

God watch over all those poor fans who died at Ibrox that day and the young lad at Shawfield stadium, all going to watch their team that day never to return. I was actually at the match that day but I was at the Celtic end that day and never knew of the disaster till later that night when I got back to a pub and saw the TV news outside the Central station as I was getting the train back to London that night. Its when tragic events like this happen that it puts life into perspective doesn't it, no matter what team you support.

That long hot summer of 1976

Do you remember that long hot summer of 1976 when it seemed it would never rain again !! well I had actually just came back form Australia after living and working there as a young bricklayer [aged 28] for two years I had spent one year in Sydney and the other year in Melbourne, I landed back in Spring of the year and had plenty a money. I landed back in London first as I had been working and living there for almost six years beforehand and wanted to see if my old girlfriend was still about.

Cut a long story short she was and we decided to get together again [yes, living in sin]. I went back to Glasgow for a week to see Ma and Da and slip them a bit of money before I blew it all, $8.000 Australian dollars I had accumulated.

So any way after a week back hame I went back down to London to live with Maggie again and start work. There was so much work for bricklayers all the way through the 70's that I never thought it would end. I could pick and choose what building sites that I wanted to work on as there was so much work about.

Now I thought with all the sunshine that I had worked in underneath the Australian sky I would have been well used to it but it was a different heat in the land of Oz to that in London.

You knew every day all through the summer that it was going to be another scorcher and I'm sure it was the same back in Glasgow and indeed the rest of Britain. There were lots of days in that long hot summer that the mortar was drying up too quick to use so most days we knocked off at 12.30 or one in the afternoon as this was dinner time [or as the English say lunch time lol]. If we did go back after dinner time it would be about two in the afternoon, when the sun is at its strongest and hottest, so nine out of ten times we just stayed in the pub, of course closing times in the pubs in London then was three o'clock in the afternoon but us crafty bricklayers had pubs lined up that would carry on serving beer in the back room until opening time of 5.30 in the evening.

I was young and fit then and could drink all day long without it really affecting me. So rather than slave out in the hot sun we drank from say one o'clock till about 6. 30 pm that's when I went home to Maggie who would have a lovely salad ready for me. Of course when we got paid we only got paid five half days but the money was that good for bricklayers back then that after giving Maggie housekeeping money I still had plenty of money left.

I must say that I loved the sunshine and just had a pair of shorts, sannies and a sloppy Joe [T-Shirt] on all the time at work. We had Abba singing all the its in 76 and Rod Stuart etc and life for me was pure magic but of course come the end of August the heatwave ended and we were back to normal working hours again but what a heatwave and what a summer never to be forgotten. I know that people who lived through that long hot summer will never forget it in a hurry too.

The Shows

Who can ever forget the thrill of walking over to the shows at Glasgow green [football pitches was where they were situated] before you got near to there you could hear the noise of the people and the sound of the pop records of the day being belted out from different stalls.

The screams of the girls as they were sitting on the motor bikes with their boyfriends or the big dipper and the guy on the Housey Housey stall shouting out "hurry up" the next game starts in 5 minutes.

The candy floss and toffee apple stall for the weans [big and small weans lol]. The coconut shy stall where you threw rubber balls to dismantle the coconut from its place but you never did !!.

Just walking round from stall to stall was dead brilliant listening to everybody chattering away. The big wheel , the ghost train. Madame Za Za who told your fortune for a shilling or was it two shillings back then in the 50/60's. Loads of teddy boys in their drainpipe troosers and velvet collared drape jackets with their teddy girls by their side trying to look "tough" and gang members of the Tongs, Brigton Derry and Cumbie all giving each other the eye but thankfully there was always a couple of cops walking about so the gangs never really fought.

My wee granny's favourite stall was where you rolled a penny down a wee wooden chute and if it landed in a square you could get three or four times your money back. It was a wonderful time and even if you never had any money to spend you could stand for ages watching all the Waltzers spinning round and around. You could spend all night there and if you were lucky and had some money left you could buy a poke of chips from the van on your way home with plenty of salt and vinegar sprinkled over them.

People from the soo-side and Brigton were lucky as they could walk home back to their tenement. Great memories to look back on, I think they still have the shows at Glasgow green but not a patch on how they used to be eh.

Govan Shipyards

Scotland was once the shipbuilder to the world and the heart of its industry was sited on the south bank of the River Clyde in the Glasgow district of Govan.

It was the famous Fairfield yard which took the Upper Clyde to great heights and worldwide prominence.

The yard was founded in 1864 by William Elder, a talented marine engineer who developed the compound engine which transformed shipbuilding by allowing vessels to use fuel more efficiently and travel further.

Under William Pearce from 1888, the company flourished, building luxurious ocean liners, steamers and naval ships for the world.

At its peak before World War 1, the Fairfield shipyard was part of a local industry which directly employed 70,000 workers in 19 yards.

The largest crane in the world, with a maximum lift capacity of 250 tons, was built at the Govan yard in 1911 and in the following year Fairfield had 12 ships under construction at the same time.

The inter-war years saw a gradual decline but Clydeside's largest shipyard still built many famous ships and during wartime it was a major builder for the Royal Navy.

But after World War 2, the decline set in swiftly and despite a major modernisation programme in the 1950s the yards of the Clyde were unable to compete with new shipbuilding superpowers such as Japan.

By 1967 the receivers were called in and it looked as if the end had come for Fairfield and for shipbuilding in Govan.

Sean Connery, at the height of his James Bond fame, made a documentary about problems besetting the yard, entitled The Bowler and the Bunnet.

Among the footage of a community on the edge of oblivion was Connery riding a bicycle around empty shipyard fabrication sheds.

The UK government's response to the crisis was to create the Upper Clyde Shipbuilders (UCS) in 1968, which had about 8,500 workers in five yards - Fairfield's and Stephens on the south bank, Connel's and Yarrow's on the north bank, and John Brown's at Clydebank.

In 1971 UCS went into receivership and was refused a government loan. This led to one of the most famous episodes in industrial history - the work-in.

The unions, led by Jimmy Reid and Jimmy Airlie, occupied the yard and made a demand of the then Conservative prime minister Edward Heath for the "right to work".

In February 1972, the government agreed to retain two yards, Yarrow at Scotstoun and Fairfield's at Govan.

Fairfield's was formed into Govan Shipbuilders in 1972, which was itself later nationalised and subsumed into British Shipbuilders in 1977.

The government of Margaret Thatcher broke up British Shipbuilders and denationalised it in 1988, when the former Fairfield yard was sold to the Norwegian Kvaerner group.

Kvaerner took the yard through another modernisation programme to enable it to specialise in the construction of liquefied natural gas and chemical tankers.

But in the late 1990s, the market became depressed and the yard had to find alternative contracts.

The yard passed to BAE Systems in 1999 and has found work over the past decade making destroyers and aircraft carriers for the Royal Navy.

BAE is a key partner in the construction of the two Queen Elizabeth class aircraft carriers being built at the Portsmouth yard and in Scotland.

However, after their construction is complete, there is only expected to be the need for one centre for naval shipbuilding in the UK to build the next generation of Type 26 frigates.

The Clyde aircraft carrier work is due to finish in 2015. It is still not clear where Type 26 frigates will be built. There are no other orders on books.

Could the sun be setting on a long tradition of Govan shipbuilding?

Who would have thought years ago that this would happen to the once mighty ship building on the Clyde??

Chapter 7

Jokes/Songs

Jokes

[1]

So here it is again !!

jokes that only work with a Glaswegian accent.

Man has a look in the bakers window, then enters the shop
he says to the baker

" Is that a doughnut, or a merangue ? "

" No " says the Baker

" Ye wur right the first time, its a doughnut"

[2]

Really old one from my schooldays......

Wee Glesca wumman goes intae a butchershop, where the butcher has
just come out of the freezer, and is standing hands behind his back,
with his rear end aimed at an electric fire.

The wee wumman checks out the display case then asks, "Is that yer
Ayrshire bacon?"

"Naw," replies the butcher. "It's jist ma haun's Ah'm heatin'."

[3]

Okay.....Only cos ah love this wan ye's will huv tae put up wae me
again..

101

Hector an wife upsterrs, lights oot an heavy snorin...CHAP CHAP at door....Hector gets up, wraps the dressin goon oan an runs doonsterrs...Opens door an therrs yer man sayin "pal kin ye gie me a push?" Astonished an pissed aff intae the bargain, homeowner then goes intae "Do you have any idea of the time here Sir? It's half past two and I have an early rise for work and I don't appreciate you rousing us from sleep"...Slams the door an huffs back uptae bed.. Who was that? asks the wife...Aw just someone who needs a push and I told them the hour etc...Oh Hector said the wife, I cannot believe you couldn't help them, have you no memory of when we were alone with the three kids in the middle of the night, car broke down and thank God for that good samaritan who helped us in our hour of need...."Oh you're sooo right dear, how thoughtless of me" said Hector beltin oot the bed an makin his way to the door again...As he opened it he shouted in earnest...Friend...Are you still there? Do you still need that push?....Aye came the reply....Well where are you friend shouted Hector....Ower here replied friend...Oan the swings!! 😂😂

[4]

A guy walks into a Glasgow pub, walks up to the bar and says to the barman a pint a lager Jimmy, Barman pulls the pint and takes the money. The guy downs his pint in a wanner then has a pee against the bar. Right so the barman does his nut shouting oot "hey you get oot a here your barred" The punter says oh I'm very sorry, I really am, I feel so embarrassed. The barman says embarrassed, you want to see a psychiatrist pal.

Anyway 18 months go by and the same punter walks into the same pub with the same barman at the bar. The barman says right you get oot a here I told you that you're barred. Then the guy says naw I don't want a drink , I jist came into thank you. The barman says you want to thank me and the punters says aye, see I took your advice, saw a pyshciatrist and now I'm cured.

Well the barman says I'm glad to hear it, do you know just to show no hard feelings I'll buy you a pint a lager. The punter downs the pint in a wanner and has a pee against the bar, Aw hey you the barman says , you said you were cured and the punter says but I am, I am, I don't feel embarrassed any more.

[5]

A wee Glesga guy fae the shipyards always wanted to go to Moscow on holiday but was too scared to fly. Eventually he decides he will go by train so he goes to the station and asks the teller for a ticket to Moscow. The ticket seller tells him I can't give you a ticket to Moscow, I'll give you a ticket to London and you can continue from there. He gets to London and asks for a ticket to Moscow, same response, can't give you a ticket to Moscow, will give you a ticket to Paris and you can continue from there. When he gets to Paris he asks for a ticket to Moscow and receives one, so he gets to the Russian capital. He has the most wonderful holiday and eventually he has to return home. He goes to the station in Moscow and asks for a ticket to Glasgow, the teller says 'Central or Queen Street'.

[6]

A pigeon from George Square in Glasgow was boasting to one from Central Station about how often he managed to "bless" the people passing by.

"Whit's your score rate?" it asked. Its pal replied *"Ach, I don't know, Aboot wan in three, mebbe, They pedestrians have taken tae runnin' lately."* The first pigeon responded *"Huh! Doon in George Square I hit seven oota ten, nae bother."*

His pal was unimpressed. *"That's nae great shakes. If I had all them big-heided cooncillors strollin' in an oot o' the City Chambers, I'd score ten oota ten every time."*

Notice in a Sauchiehall Street, Glasgow, restaurant - *"Kids - eat two for the price of one..."* to which a passing non-customer had added *"I can't eat a whole child, far less two..."*

Glasgow teachers are known to use the following translations for the remarks they make on pupils' report cards:
"A born leader" - *Runs a protection racket*
"Easy-going" - *Bone idle*
"Good progress" - *You should have seen him a year ago*
"Friendly" - *Never shuts up*
"Helpful" - *A creep*
"Reliable" - *Informs on his friends*
"Expresses himself confidently" - *Impertinent*
"Enjoys physical education" - *A bully*
"Does not accept authority easily" - *Dad is in prison*
"Often appears tired" - *Stays up all night watching television*
"A rather solitary child" - *He smells*
"Popular in the playground" - *Sells pornography*

Sandy and his friend Angus lived in identical tenement flats in Glasgow. One night at the pub Sandy mentioned he had just papered the kitchen. Angus said, *"I've been wanting tae dae that! How much paper did ye get?"*
"Seven rolls," said Sandy. A week later they met again and Angus says, *"Here you! I had two and a half rolls of paper left over frae my kitchen."*
"Aye", says Sandy, *"So did I."*

104

"Heaven seems very little improvement on Glesga" a Glasgow man is said to have murmured after his death to a friend who had predeceased him. *"Man, this is not Heaven,"* the other replied.

~~~~~~

How do you know when you're staying in Glasgow? When you call the hotel desk and say *"I've gotta leak in my sink"* and the response is *"go ahead"*.

~~~~~~

Glaswegians consider Edinburgh to be in the east - the Far East. Edinburghers consider Glasgow to be in the west - the Wild West.

~~~~~~

The only plumber in Glasgow to charge reasonable fees died and was sent to Hell by mistake. Eventually it was realised in Heaven that there was an honest Glaswegian plumber in the wrong place so Saint Peter telephoned (on the hot line) to Satan.
"Have you got an honest plumber there?"
"Yes."
"He's ours, so can you send him up?"
"You can't have him!"
"Why not?"
"Because he's the only one who understands air conditioning. It's really cool down here now."
"Send him up at once," shouted Saint Peter, *"or we'll sue."*
"You'll sue?" laughed the voice at the other end. *"And where will you get hold of a lawyer in Heaven?"*

Songs

The Bell , the bell the B E L L, tell the teacher ah'm no well
If you're late shut the gate, don't come back till hawf past 8

~~~~~~

Mah Maw's a millionaire, blue eyes and curly hair
See her walking doon the street wae her big banana feet
Hiv a banana

Sitting among the Eskimos
playing a game a dominoes
Hiv a banana

She stoats mah Faither aff the wa
Like a wee capeechi baw
Hiv a banana

~~~~~~

Not last night but the night before
Three wee monkeys came to the door

Wan wae a fiddle , wan wae a drum
And wan wae a pancake stuck tae his bum

~~~~~~

Ah went tae the pictures the morra
Took a seat jist like that

Ah said tae the wummin behind me
Ah canny see fur yer hat

She gave me some broken biscuits
Ah ate them then gave them back

Ah fell fae the stalls tae the balcony
And broke a front bone in mah back

~~~~~~

PK chewing gum
A penny a packet

First you chew it
Then you crack it

Then you stick it in yer jacket

PK chewing gum
A penny a packet.

~~~~~~

Murder murder Polisman three stairs up
The wumman in the middle door hit me wae a cup

Mah nose is aw bleedin, my eye's aw cut
Murder murder Polisman three stairs up

~~~~~~

Get a TV

At a coffee bar in Byres Road in Glasgow's smart West End, young
Shona and her friends were discussing what the "ideal partner" would
be like. Shona launched into her description (having clearly given a
lot of thought to the subject). *"The man I marry must be entertaining
amongst company and be smart and intelligent. He must be musical.
Tell jokes so that I laugh - and so do others. He should be able to sing
romantic songs. And - of course - stay home at night!"* A grey-haired

woman at the next table looked over and commented: *"Lassie, if that's all you want, get a TV..."*

~~~~~~

It's a Girl...

Like all good, modern fathers, Geordie was present when his wife gave birth to their first child. *"It's a girl!"* declared the midwife - and then noticed the slightly crestfallen look on Geordie's face. *"Are you disappointed that it's a girl?"* she asked. Geordie tried to cover up and replied: *"Not really. A girl was my second choice...."*

~~~~~~

Recipe for a Good Marriage

Tavish McTavish was a stranger to the Auchenshuggle Arms but told the assembled gathering that he was approaching his 50th wedding anniversary and his wife and he rarely had an argument.. When asked for his secret for a happy married life he replied *"Well, I've tried to treat her well, spend money on her, tell her that's she the best wife a man ever had, but the best thing I ever did was to take her to Italy for our 20th wedding anniversary."* Someone asked what he was planning to do for their 50th wedding anniversary, to which Tavish replied *"I'm going back to Italy - to collect her and bring her back...."*

~~~~~~

Breakfast in Bed

Hector remarked to his wife *"You know, Morag, I really miss you serving me breakfast in bed..."* Morag looked at her middle-aged husband in disbelief. *"But I never gave you breakfast in bed!"* Her husband nodded and replied: *"Yes, I know. I just said that I missed it..."* (They say that Hector will make a full recovery once he leaves hospital).

~~~~~~

Night Out
Dugald suggested to his wife that they should go out for the evening and have some fun and enjoyment. His wife agreed immediately and then remarked *"If you get home before I do, leave the hallway lights on...."*

~~~~~

Change for the Better?
Angus had been married for six months and was chatting to his friend about married life. *"Ever since I got married, my wife has tried to change me. In the last six months I've stopped drinking, smoking, staying out till all hours and I now dress well, enjoy classical music, enjoy fine food and wine and now invest money instead of spending it all. But I'm sad. I now realise that I am so improved, my wife isn't good enough for me any more..."*

~~~~~

Good Tip
Sadie and her husband used the same desk-top PC but she was getting fed up with her spouse reading her e-mails. Then a friend (who had the same problem) gave her a tip that stopped the intrusion dead in its tracks. She renamed the mail folder "Instruction Manuals" and he never went near it again.

~~~~~

A Proposal
McTavish had been going out with Morag for about two years. Eventually, he decided to "pop the question". As the couple sat in a car, watching the sun go down, McTavish collected enough courage to ask her the most momentous of all questions: *"There are quite a lot of advantages to being a bachelor,"* he began, *"but there comes a time when a man needs companionship of another being - someone who will regard him as perfect, as an idol, who will be kind and faithful when times are hard, and who will share life's joys and sorrows."*

McTavish thought he saw a sympathetic gleam in Morag's eyes. To his delight, she nodded in agreement. Finally, she responded, *"I think its a great idea! Yes, I can help you choose which puppy to buy..."*

~~~~~

Not Tactful - 1
Effie looked up at her husband and said *"You're not yourself today.....I noticed the improvement immediately."*

Not Tactful - 2
Donald was being accused by his wife of not listening and snapped back *"I'm ready to listen...are you ready to think?"*

~~~~~

Diamonds are a Girl's Best Friend?
Angus was boasting to his friend about the ring of large, sparkling diamonds he had given to his wife for her birthday. His friend was impressed - but a little puzzled - and asked *"I thought she wanted one of those red Ferrari sports cars?"* Angus looked scathingly at his friend and replied: *"Yes, she did want that - but where was I going to find a fake Ferrari?"*

~~~~~

Family Dispute
Davie McFlannel became alarmed at the sounds of shouting and fighting in the house next door and eventually phoned the police. The police responded about two hours later - expecting that things would have calmed down by then. But the noise of crockery breaking and thumps and bangs suggested that the fighting was still in progress. The police constable knocked loudly on the door and eventually a disheveled woman answered the door. The policeman demanded to know *"Who's head of the family here?"* and was promptly told: *"Just wait there another five minutes - I'm settling that right now."*

110

~~~~~~~

Two Glesga men decide to join the foreign Legion and soon find themselves in a Foreign Legion fort in the middle of the desert, anyway it was midnight and they were on sentry duty on the battlements of the fort.

When across from them an other Foreign Legion soldier shouts out at the top of his voice "Arabs coming" so Jimmy wan of the Glesga boys shoots him dead, his pal Boaby says whit the hell did you shoot him fur and Jimmy says, there's only wan thing in this world that I hate more than Arabs and his pal says"whits that", a bloody grass says Jimmy.

~~~~~~~

Man walks into a tailors shop and says to the assistant I want a "Maroon jaiket", the assistant says a "Maroon jaiket" Sir ?
The man says aye to fit" mah roon" shooders

~~~~~~~

A wee guy walks into a green-grocers shop and says to the assistant, I want a tin a pigeons. The assistant says "sorry no can do"

Chapter 8

Photos

Glasgow Queen St station

What a wonderful view of that famous glass arched dome-roof covering Queen street railway station, it was partially hidden over the years with the building in front of it.

Now that building has been demolished we can once again see it, how many times have we passed through this railway station on our way to catch a train and never stopped to look up and this magnificent glass arched roof.

Sometimes in my younger years I would use the station as a short cut through to Georges square or going the other way as a short cut to Jacksons dog house pub in Dundas street as it was a great pub for bricklayers to meet up in and as being a bricklayer myself you could keep track of where all the work was for us bricklayers. If you look at the banner to your right you will see the wording "People make Glasgow" and that is spot on, we are a very down to earth folk who like a good laugh. I have to say I am glad that I was born in Glasgow with its great people and fine buildings.

Glasgow Central station

The busiest railway station in Glasgow [and Scotland] and it was here in 1968 that I first set out on my travels as a bricklayer that would take me halfway round the world. Every time I land back in the central station and step off of the train from London [where I now live] the electricity runs up my legs as if to say Danny son you're back hame. Always a busy station with plenty of eating places and shops, oh and a few Glesga pigeons too. Its changed days from years ago when I was a 13 year old train spotter in 1961 and the station still had the steam engines pulling in, yes its much cleaner now. Do you remember at the Glasgow fair fortnight and on the first Saturday there used to be thousands of people queueing up with their suitcases going away for the "fair". In those days the suitcases we have today with wheels on it to pull it along easily had not been invented. So your Ma and Da would be on the look-out for one of the many "porters" that were on duty on the concourse to assist you carrying your luggage to the train and of course he was always given "a tip".

The Odeon

The Odeon picture house in Renfield street must hold so many happy memories for us Glaswegians and not only as a picture house but also as music stage to watch all the top singing artists and groups over the years. I clearly remember in 1964 watching Roy Orbison live on stage there. I'm sure thousands [if not millions] of fans saw the Beatles, Tom Jones etc etc over the years, it really was the "in place" for the music scene back in the day. Well I'm glad to say that it has been revamped now and looks real good from the outside. I have a personal story to tell about the Odeon, it was way back in 1967 and I took my girlfriend Rena there on a Wednesday night to see the film "The Swiss Family Robinson" starring John Mills, Dorothy McGuire, James MacArthur etc. I took Rena by the arm and walked into the foyer and went to the ticket office to buy our tickets, after I got our tickets I took Rena by the arm and walked her to go into the cinema but Rena was standing in front of me, how could this be? Seems I had taken another young lady's arm by mistake. Oh what a Riddy, and if looks could have killed then I would have been a goner!! Needless to say there was no back seat winchin that night!!!

The Argyll Arcade

This is one of Europe's oldest covered shopping arcades and Scotland's first ever shopping mall. This L shaped arcade was built in 1827 in the Parisian style and the arcade was cut through old tenements and provided a link between Buchanan st and Argyle st. So many fine jewellers shops to choose an engagement ring or high class watch etc from and not forgetting the famous Sloan's bar. Not forgetting the Clyde model dockyard shop for scale model trains etc. Two flights of stairs and an old fashioned lift takes you up to the the floor above which has more jewellers shops. Even if you don't intend to buy anything it's wonderful just to take a stroll through the arcade and admiringly look at what's on sale. While at either entrance to the arcade you have a very well dressed gentleman [paid for by the shops ?] to give you any info about the shops. Maybe like me you thought that the Argyll arcade was spelt "Argyle arcade" see I'm always learning about Glasgow !! after being away 51 years.

The Pavilion Theatre

One of Glasgow's oldest theatres the Pavilion theatre of varieties opened on the 29th of February 1904 as a music hall. Many of the leading music hall artistes of the early 20th century appeared at the Pavilion including Marie Llyod, Little Tich, Harry Lauder, Sarah Bernhardt and the then unknown Charlie Chaplin. In 1920 the Pavilion started producing pantomimes and still continues to produce pantomimes. The Pavilion theatre is now the only privately run theatres in Scotland and one of a few unsubsidised independent theatres left in Britain outside London. In 2004 Janette Krankie was seriously injured during a performance of Jack and the beanstalk at the theatre, but made a full recovery. In 2007 the Pavilion theatre reinvented itself as the Scottish national theatre of variety with a launch including numerous stars of the stage and the announcement was made by Iain Gordon the general manger. The location of the theatre is at the top of Renfield street, at the corner of Renfrew street and a block away from the Royal Scottish Conservatoire. It is a short walk from Cowcaddens and Buchanan street subway and Buchanan bus station.

117

The Hielanman's Umbrella

The Hielanman's umbrella is a landmark in Glasgow city, it's the local Glaswegian nickname for the glass walled railway bridge which carries the platforms of Glasgow central station across Argyle street. Due to the forced displacement of people during the second phase of the Highland clearances in the 19th century, 30,000 Highlanders who spoke Scottish Gaelic but no English, came to Glasgow to find work. When arriving in the city they were housed in many different areas of Glasgow. Over many years Highlanders continued to arrive and began to keep in touch by meeting under the bridge, mostly at weekends. With Glasgow's inclement weather they would meet under the bridge to keep out of the rain and so it became known as the meeting place for Heilanmen or rather Heilanman's umbrella [to stay dry]. Looking at the photo above I see Grants public house to the right hand side where many a time I had a pint as a young man. Also the corner shop with red lettering used to be Burton's the tailor shop where I used to get my suits made to measure.

The Southern Necropolis

The Southern Necropolis is a cemetery in the Gorbals district of southern Glasgow. It was opened in the year 1840 to provide an affordable and respectable place of burial for the people of the Gorbals and the surrounding areas of the city of Glasgow. Over 250.000 individuals have been buried within the many lairs. The cemetery was established in response to the crowded state of the old Gorbals burial ground on Rutherglen rd. Proposals for a new cemetery were put forward in 1839 and the following year land was purchased from William Gilmour of Oatlands. The first burial, that of a 16 month - old child took place on 21 st of July 1840. There are three sections to the cemetery, central opened in 1840, eastern in 1846 and the larger western section opened in 1850. Myself as a wean used to play in the Southern Necropolis with my pals and were always on the look out for "Vampires". I only lived a 5 minute walk away in Fauldhouse st. It has been my pleasure to donate my royalty payments from my books over the years to help with the upkeep/promotion of the graveyard ran by my good pal Colin Mackie and his wife Elsie and all the other good folk who do such great work alongside them.

Templetons on the green

Templetons on the green was previously known as the Templeton carpet factory, a very distinctive building close to the people's palace. This building opened in 1892, in 1984 it was converted into the Templeton business centre, then in 2005 a major regeneration project made it into a mixed use "lifestyle village" incorporating apartments, office spaces and the WEST brewery, bar and restaurant. The building was designed and built as a carpet factory for James Templeton and son, for the manufacture of Templeton's patented spool axminster carpets. After repeated design proposals had been rejected by Glasgow corporation, James Templeton hired the famous architect William Leiper to produce a design that would be so grand it could not possibly be rejected. So William modelled the building on the Doges Palace in Venice [Venetian Gothic style]. During its construction in 1889 the factory facade collapsed killing 29 women. The building was completed in 1892 and is an eye catching building with its many different colours.

Trongate

Trongate is one of the oldest streets in the city of Glasgow, Trongate begins at Glasgow cross where the Tolbooth steeple is situated, which was the the original centre of medieval Glasgow. It goes westwards, changing its name to Argyle street at Glassford street. Previously known as St Thenew's Gait [the way to the supposed site of St Thenew's burial] it was around the start of the 1500s that the name Trongate first began to be used. The name comes by virtue of a weigh-beam erected in the mid -16th century, used for all goods requiring to be weighed for duty reasons, including from early shipping on the Clyde. Tron is a Scots word of Norman origin for weighing scales. The Trongate was one of the areas which was affected by a large fire on17[th] of June 1652, which destroyed a third of the town and left around 1.000 families homeless. The Tron Church was founded as the Collegiate Church of Our Lady and St Ann's in 1525 by James Houston. It became a Protestant Church after the reformation.

The People's Palace and Winter gardens

The people's palace and winter gardens in Glasgow is a museum and glasshouse situated in Glasgow green and was opened on 22nd of January 1898 by the Earl of Rosebery. At the time, the east end of Glasgow was one of the most unhealthiest and overcrowded parts of the city and the peoples palace was intended to provide a cultural centre for the people. It was designed by the city engineer, Alexander B McDonald. At the opening ceremony Lord Rosebery stated "A palace of pleasure and imagination around which the people may place their affections and which may give them a home on which their memory may rest". He declared the building open to the people for ever and ever. How many of us Glaswegians have visited the two buildings in our lifetimes eh, I always remember walking over there and the two massive whale-jaw-bones at the entrance of one doorway has always stayed in my memory. Of course we nicknamed the winter palace the "hoat hoose" because of the heat inside there. Just two of Glasgow's fine structures for us to cherish.

Chapter 9

Famous Glaswegians

Jim Watt

Jim Watt, MBE was born on the 18th of July 1948 and is a former boxer and commentator who became world champion in the lightweight division when Roberto Duran left the title vacant in 1979, and the WBC had him fight Alfredo Pitalua, Watt knocked out Pitalua in twelve rounds.

Raised in the Bridgeton and Possilpark areas of Glasgow, Watt trained at Cardowan amateur boxing club in the city's Maryhill district. His father died when Jim was five years old.

He came to prominence in 1968 by beating John H Stracey to the ABA championships: he turned professional immediately afterwards, declining the chance to compete as an amateur at the 1968 summer Olympics in Mexico City.

Watt beat such notables as future world champion Sean O'Grady, former Champion Perico Fernandez, Charlie Nash and Howard Davis Jnr.

The fight with O'Grady was particularly controversial: Watt won by a knock-out in round twelve when the referee stopped the fight because of a cut suffered by O'Grady.

According to the book: "The Ring:Boxing The 20th Century", the cut was produced by a head butt, in which case the judges scorecards would have been checked and whoever was ahead given the win by a technical decision.

The referee, however, declared incorrectly that O'Grady's cut had been produced by a punch, therefore, Watt officially but unjustly won the fight by a knock-out. When O'Grady won the WBA title four months later Watt was declared lightweight champion by "The Ring"

Watt had also fought and lost to Ken Buchanan after fifteen rounds in 1973. On 20th of June 1981, he fought his last fight when losing the

WBC world lightweight title to Alexis Arguello by a fifteen round decision in London.

Watt retired with a record of 38 wins [27 by knock-out] and 8 losses [3 by knock-out]

Watt along with former middleweight champion Alan Minter, earns his living as an after dinner speaker. He was awarded an MBE, he was long -term co-commentator with Reg Gutteridge on ITV's "The big fight live " and moved with Gutteridge to Sky sports in 1996 when ITV withdrew from boxing coverage. During 2016 Watt announced his retirement as a boxing commentator.

Watt made a special guest appearance on the BBC's "Still Game" sitcom in August 2007. As well as television adverts for Kelvin Timber [a Scottish home and building supplies stores company] in the 1980's he and his family settled in the town of Kirkintilloch to the north of Glasgow.

Scotland can be very proud of our Jim Watt.

Dorothy Paul

Dorothy Paul, was born in Dennistoun Glasgow in 1937 as Dorothy Pollock and is a Scottish screen and stage actress. Comedian and entertainer. She is perhaps best known for her stage shows and live performances, most notably at the Pavilion theatre in Glasgow.

Originating from the Dennistoun area of Glasgow, she started her main career in the late 1960's, with her first credited roles in television shows such as "The revenue men", "Sutherland's law" and "Garnock way". She also featured in the film "Micheline's mother" which was presented at the 2005 film "Festival."

After many successful years with various stage performances, including Dorothy Paul live, she had many guest appearances in "Still game" and Taggart.

The Steamie
In December 1988, Paul starred as Magrit in the television adaption of the play "the Steamie" which was written by Tony Roper. In the show she featured alongside fellow cast members Eileen McCallum, Katy Murphy and Peter Mullan. The adaption is generally favoured as one of Scotland's most loved television broadcasts.

Her role in the "Steamie" featured the famous "isn't it wonderful to be a woman?" speech in which Paul delivers an explanation about the life of a woman during that area.

"Isn't it wonderful to be a woman?, you get up at the crack of dawn, you get the breakfast ready, you get the weans ready and oot the hoose looking as respectable as you can afford and you wash the dishes, finish the ironing, maybe give the floor a skite over and then you're away to yer ain wee job, maybe cleaning offices or serving in a shop or washing stairs. You finish your work and back into your hoose to mair work. What are we? We're skivvies, unpaid skivvies".

Dorothy Paul was a regular on Scottish TV in the 1980's and 90's and had her own new year programme that featured her singing and telling stories of her childhood. In the summer of 2009, Dorothy was a guest presenter on STV's daily lifestyle show "The Hour" alongside main anchor Stephen Jardine.

Comedienne and raconteur Dorothy Paul started in theatre after winning a talent competition. She joined Scottish televisions "The One O'Clock gang" in 1959. She appeared at the Butlins holiday camp from 1974 and hosted "Housecall".

She also starred in the soap opera "Garnock way" and the successful stage dramas "The Steamie" and "The Celtic story". From 1991 she became noted for her one woman shows including "Now that's her", "Now that's her again" and "The full Dorothy" demonstrating her talent for humorous observations from her childhood and her impersonations of Glasgow characters.

She currently lives in Glasgow and has expressed a keen interest in painting. She is also Patron of the Family addiction support service [FASS] a charity in Glasgow offering support services to those affected by drug and alcohol addictions.

Donovan

Born Donovan Philips Leitch on 10th of May 1946 in Maryhill Glasgow, he is a Scottish singer, songwriter and guitarist. He developed an eclectic and distinctive style that blended "folk, jazz, psychedelia and world music".

He has lived in Scotland, Hertfordshire [England], London, California and since at least 2008 in County Cork Ireland, with his family. Emerging from the British folk scene Donovan reached fame in the United Kingdom in early 1965 with live performances on the pop TV series "Ready steady Go".

Having signed with Pye records in 1965 he recorded singles and two albums in the folk vein, after which he signed to CBS/Epic records in the US- the first signing by the company's new vice president Clive Davis, and became more successful internationally.

He began a long and successful collaboration with leading British independent record producer Mickie Most, scoring multiple hit singles and albums in the UK, the US and other countries.

His most successful singles were the early UK hits "Catch the wind", "Colours" and "Universal soldier" in 1965. Then in 1966 in September "Sunshine Superman" topped America's "Billboard hot 100" chart for one week and went to number two in Britain, followed by "Mellow Yellow" at US number 2 in December 1966.
Then 1968's "Hurdy Gurdy man" in the top 5 in both countries. Then he had "Atlantis" which reached US number 7 in May 1969.

He became a friend of pop musicians including Joan Baez, Brian Jones and the Beatles. He taught John Lennon a finger picking guitar style in 1968 that Lennon employed in "Dear Prudence", "Julia", "Happiness is a warm gun" and other songs.

Donovan's commercial fortunes waned after parting with Mickie Most in 1969 and he left the industry for a time .

Donovan continued to perform and record sporadically in the 1970's and 1980's. his musical style and "hippie" image were scorned by critics, especially after "Punk rock". his performing and recording became sporadic until a revival in the 1990's with the emergence of Britain's "Rave scene".

He recorded the 1996 album "Sutras" with producer Rick Rubin and in 2004 made a new album "Beat cafe".

Donovan was inducted into the "Rock and roll hall of fame" in 2012 and "The Songwriters hall of fame" in 2014.

Allan Pinkerton

Allan Pinkerton was born in the Gorbals, Glasgow, Scotland, to William Pinkerton and his wife, Isobel McQueen, on August 25, 1819. He left school at the age of 10 after his father's death. Pinkerton read voraciously and was largely self-educated. A Cooper by trade, Pinkerton was active in the Scottish Chartist movement as a young man. He secretly married Joan Carfrae (1822-1887) from Duddingston, [then a singer], in Glasgow on 13 March 1842. Pinkerton emigrated to the United States in 1842.

Pinkerton first got interested in criminal detective work while wandering through the wooded groves around the Dundee area in the USA, looking for trees to make barrel staves, when he came across a band of counterfeiters—who may have been affiliated with the notorious Banditti of the Prairie. After observing their movements for some time he informed the local sheriff, who arrested them. This later led to Pinkerton being appointed, in 1849, as the first police detective in Chicago, Cook county, Illinois.   In 1850, he partnered with Chicago attorney Edward Rucker in forming the North-Western Police Agency, which later became Pinkerton & Co, and finally Pinkerton National Detective Agency, still in existence today as Pinkerton Consulting and Investigations, a subsidiary of Securatis AB. Pinkerton's business insignia was a wide open eye with the caption "We never sleep." As the US expanded in territory, and rail transport increased. Pinkerton's agency solved a series of train robberies during the 1850s, first bringing Pinkerton into contact with George McClellan, then Chief Engineer and Vice Prof the Illinois Central Railroad, and Abraham Lincoln, the company's lawyer.

When the Civil War began, Pinkerton served as head of the Union Intelligence Service during the first two years, heading off an alleged assassination plot in Baltimore, Maryland while guarding Abraham Lincoln on his way to Washington, D.C. as well as identifying troop numbers in military campaigns. His agents often worked undercover as Confederate soldiers and sympathizers to gather military intelligence. Pinkerton himself served on several undercover missions as a confederate soldier using the alias Major E.J. Allen. He worked across the Deep South in the summer of 1861, focusing on fortifications and Confederate plans. He was found out in Memphis and barely escaped with his life. This counter intelligence work done by Pinkerton and his agents is comparable to the work done by today's US Army counter intelligence special agents in which Pinkerton's agency is considered an early predecessor. He was succeeded as Intelligence Service chief by Lafayette Baker; the Intelligence Service was the predecessor of the US Secret service. His work led to the establishment of the Federal secret service.

Following Pinkerton's service with the Union Army, he continued his pursuit of train robbers, including the Reno gang. He was hired by the railroad express companies to track outlaw Jesse James, but after Pinkerton failed to capture him, the railroad withdrew their financial support and Pinkerton continued to track James at his own expense. After James allegedly captured and killed one of Pinkerton's undercover agents (who was working undercover at the farm neighbouring the James family's farmstead), he abandoned the chase. Some consider this failure Pinkerton's biggest defeat. He also opposed Labour unions. In 1872, the Spanish Government hired Pinkerton to help suppress a revolution in Cuba which intended to end slavery and give citizens the right to vote. If Pinkerton knew this, then it directly contradicts statements in his 1883 book *The Spy of the Rebellion*, where he professes to be an ardent abolitionist and hater of slavery. The Spanish government abolished slavery in 1880 and a Royal Decree abolished the last vestiges of it in 1886.

Allan Pinkerton died in Chicago on July 1, 1884. It is usually said that Pinkerton slipped on the pavement and bit his tongue, resulting in gangrene. Contemporary reports give conflicting causes, such as that he succumbed to a stroke (he had one a year earlier) or to Malaria, which he had contracted during a trip to the Southern United States. At the time of his death, he was working on a system to centralize all criminal identification records, a database now maintained by the federal Bureau of Investigation. Pinkerton was a lifelong atheist. Pinkerton is buried in Graceland Cemetry, Chicago. He is a member of the Military Intelligence Hall of Fame.

Jimmy Reid

James Reid (9 July 1932 – 10 August 2010) was a Scottish trade union activist, orator, politician and journalist born in Govan, Glasgow. His role as spokesman and one of the leaders in the Upper Clyde shipbuilders work-in between June 1971 and October 1972 attracted international recognition. He later served as Rector of the University of Glasgow, and subsequently became a journalist and broadcaster. Formerly a member of the Communist party of Great Britain, Reid was later a Labour party member. After supporting the Scottish Socialist party in the late 1990s, he joined the Scottish National party in 2005 and fully supported Scottish independence. He died in 2010 after a long illness.

Reid was born in Govan, Glasgow, then a major British shipbuilding centre. In his youth, Reid joined the Young Communist league and was later a member of the Communist party of Great Britain. He was involved in organising a major apprentices' strike at the Clyde shipyards in 1951.

Reid came to prominence in the early 1970s, when he led the Upper Clyde shipbuilding work-in to try to stop Edward Heath's conservative Government from closing down the shipyards on the River Clyde.

That government had decided that the shipyards should operate without state subsidy, which would have resulted in at least six thousand job losses. An engineer by trade and shop-steward of the Amalgamated union of engineering workers, Reid, along with his colleagues Jimmy Airlie, Sammy Gilmore and Sammy Barr decided that the best way to show the viability of keeping the yards open was by staging a 'work-in' rather than by going on strike. This meant that the workers would continue to complete what orders the shipyard had until the government changed policy

In a famous speech given to the workers, Reid announced the beginning of workers' control of the shipyard and insisted on self-discipline while this was in force:
"We are not going to strike. We are not even having a sit-in strike. Nobody and nothing will come in and nothing will go out without our permission.

And there will be no hooliganism, there will be no vandalism, there will be no bevvy-ing because the world is watching us, and it is our responsibility to conduct ourselves with responsibility, and with dignity, and with maturity".

John Lennon and Billy Connolly and members of the public providing donations. The campaign was successful in persuading Heath to back down the following year, and the Clyde shipyards received £101 million in public support over the next three years.

He was elected as a Communist councillor in Clydebank, where, prior to the local government reform of the mid-1970s, there were a few Communist councillors.

He stood for the Communist party of Great Britain in East Dunbartonshire in the 1970 general election.

Reid also served as Rector of the University of Glasgow, elected in 1971, largely on the back of his union activities. When installed as Rector, he gave a critically acclaimed speech, which became known as "the rat-race speech". The New York Times printed the speech in full and described it as "the greatest speech since President Lincoln's Gettysburg Address.

"Reject the values and false morality that underlie these attitudes. A rat race is for rats. We're not rats. We're human beings. Reject the insidious pressures in society that would blunt your critical faculties to all that is happening around you, that would caution silence in the face of injustice lest you jeopardise your chances of promotion and self-advancement. This is how it starts and before you know where you are, you're a fully paid-up member of the rat-pack. The price is

133

too high. It entails the loss of your dignity and human spirit. Or as Christ put it, "What doth it profit a man if he gain the whole world and suffer the loss of his soul?"

Around 1975, Reid left the Communist Party. The breakaway Scottish Labour party considered recruiting him, but its leader Jim Sillars said: "If we have that chap in he'll be taking time away from me on the box".

About a year after he left the CP, Reid joined the Labour party . He was their candidate in Dundee east in 1979, but lost to then Scottish National party (SNP) leader Gordon Wilson. The decision by Dundee East Constituency Labour party to select him as their candidate was controversial, as he had been a party member for less than the two years normally expected.

He is sometimes referred to as "the best MP Scotland never had".

Reid continued to support Labour up until the 1997 General election, but thereafter became disillusioned with the New Labour phenomenon. In 1998, he urged people to support the Scottish Socialist party (SSP) in the first elections to the new Scottish parliament.

In the 2004 SNP leadership contest, he urged SNP members to support Alex Salmond for leader and Nicola Sturgeon for deputy leader, and he joined the party in the following year.

In 2007, a play by the writer Brian McGeachan about Reid's life was performed. Entitled *From Govan to Gettysburg*, it starred John Cairney and toured as part of Jimmy Reid's 75th birthday celebrations.

Reid retired to Rothesay on the Isle of Bute. On 10 August 2010, Reid died at Inverclyde Royal hospital He had suffered a brain haemorrhage earlier in the week and had been in poor health for a number of years.

After a private service in Rothesay on the Isle of Bute, his hearse was driven into Glasgow for a secular funeral service at the Govan old Parish Church on 19 August.

The cortege passed the BAE Systems Surface ships yard in Govan, one of the Shipyards saved after the collapse of UCS, where hundreds of workers had gathered outside in tribute. The funeral service at Govan Old was attended by notable figures including Ed Balls, Ed Milliband, Gordon Brown, Alex Salmond, Sir Alex Ferguson and Sir Billy Connolly.

He was survived by his wife Joan, three daughters and three granddaughters, one of whom, Joani Reid is a Labour Party Councillor in the London Borough of Lewisham The left-wing think tank and advocacy group, the Jimmy Reid Foundation, was established in his memory by the Editorial Board of the Scottish left review.

Jimmy Reid = "Reflections of a Clyde built man" [souvenier press]

Lena Martell

Lena Martell (born **Helen Thomson**; 15 May 1940, Possilpark, Glasgow) is a Scottish singer, with a long career in theatre, televison and musicals. She has recorded thirty albums which include the number one UK single with "One day at a time" in 1979

She began singing at the age of 11 with her eldest brother's band. She became a singer for the Jimmie McGregor Band at the Barrowland Ballroom, Glasgow. After his untimely death, she decided to pursue a career in music as a tribute She released a number of standards in the 1970s on the Pye record label, drew crowds at cabarets and concert halls and became a major recording star with silver, gold and platinum awards. Her cover of the song "One Day at a Time", written by Marijohn Wilkin and Kris Kristofferson, reached the top of the UK singles chart for three weeks in November 1979. She placed six albums in the UK albums chart between 1974 and 1980, including four that reached the Top 20

In the 1970 and 80s her Saturday Night TV shows for BBC UK ran over a period of ten years, with evening audiences of over 12 million.

Moving to the USA she sang in New York and Las Vegas with Frank Sinatra, Sammy Davies junior and others and toured the world performing in concert halls. She has starred in musicals in Broadway, first when deputising for Barbara Streisand, and headlining in London's West End theatres.

Her successes at London Palladium equalled the box office of Shirley Maclaine and Bette Midler. Although out of the limelight for a period while nursing her sick mother, Martell has now returned to the music industry and is still touring the UK. She has lately released a few albums on the Scot-Disc label. Her double album *One Day at a Time: An Anthology of Song* was released on Castle Records in 2003

Martell has had surgery to replace a valve in her heart, and in March 2008 underwent a triple heart bypass operation.

Charles Rennie Mackintosh

Charles Rennie Mackintosh was born at 70 Parson Street, Townhead, Glasgow, on 7 June 1868, the fourth of eleven children and second son of William Mackintosh, a superintendent and chief clerk of the City of Glasgow Police, he and his wife, Margaret Rennie. Mackintosh grew up in the old Townhead and Dennistoun (Firpark Terrace) areas of Glasgow, and he attended Reid's Public School and the Allen Glen's Institution.

In 1890 Mackintosh was the second winner of the Alexander Thomson Travelling Studentship, set up for the "furtherance of the study of ancient classic architecture, with special reference to the principles illustrated in Mr. Thomson's works."

He started work with the Honeyman & Keppie architectural practice where he started his first major architectural project which was the Glasgow Herald building [now known as the Lighthouse]. He was engaged to marry his employer's sister, Jessie Keppie.

Around 1892, Mackintosh met fellow artist Margaret MacDonald at the Glasgow School of Art. He and fellow student Herbert MacNair, also an apprentice at Honeyman and Keppie, were introduced to Margaret and her sister Frances MacDonald by the head of the Glasgow School of Art, Francis Henry Newbery, who saw similarities in their work. Margaret and Charles married on 22 August 1900. The couple had no children. MacNair and Frances also married the previous year. The group worked collaboratively and came to be known as "The Four", and were prominent figures in Glasgow style art and design.

In 1904, after he had completed several successful building designs, Mackintosh became a partner in Honeyman & Keppie, and the company became Honeyman, Keppie & Mackintosh. When economic hardships were causing many architectural practices to close, in 1913, he resigned from the partnership and attempted to open his own practice.

Mackintosh lived most of his life in the city of Glasgow, located on the banks of the River Clyde. During the Industrial Revolutionl the city had one of the greatest production centres of heavy engineering and shipbuilding in the world. As the city grew and prospered, a faster response to the high demand for consumer goods and arts was necessary. Industrialized, mass-produced items started to gain popularity. Along with the Industrial Revolution, Asian style and emerging modernist ideas also influenced Mackintosh's designs. When the Japanese isolationist regime softened, they opened themselves to globalisation resulting in notable Japanese influence around the world. Glasgow's link with the eastern country became particularly close with shipyards at the River Clyde being exposed to Japanese navy and training engineers. Japanese design became more accessible and gained great popularity. In fact, it became so popular and so incessantly appropriated and reproduced by Western artists, that the Western world's fascination and preoccupation with Japanese art gave rise to the new term, Japonism or Japonisme.

At the same time a new philosophy concerned with creating functional and practical design was emerging throughout Europe: the so-called "modernist ideas". The main concept of the Modernist movement was to develop innovative ideas and new technology: design was concerned with the present and the future, rather than with history and tradition. Heavy ornamentation and inherited styles were discarded. Even though Mackintosh became known as the 'pioneer' of the movement, his designs were far removed from the bleak utilitarianism of Modernism. His concern was to build around the needs of people: people seen, not as masses, but as individuals who needed not a machine for living in but a work of art. Mackintosh took his inspiration from his Scottish upbringing and blended them with the flourish of Art Nouveau and the simplicity of Japanese forms.

While working in architecture, Charles Rennie Mackintosh developed his own style: a contrast between strong right angles and floral-inspired decorative motifs with subtle curves (for example, the Mackintosh Rose motif), along with some references to traditional Scottish architecture. The project that helped make his international

138

reputation was the Gkasgow school of Art (1897–1909). During the early stages of the Glasgow School of Art Mackintosh also completed the Queens Cross Church projectt in Maryhill, Glasgow. This is considered to be one of Mackintosh's most mysterious projects. It is the only church by the Glasgow-born artist to be built and is now the Charles Rennie Mackintosh Society headquarters. Like his contemporary Frank Llyod Wright, Mackintosh's architectural designs often included extensive specifications for the detailing, decoration, and furnishing of his buildings. The majority, if not all, of this detailing and significant contributions to his architectural drawings were designed and detailed by his wife Margaret Macdonald whom Charles had met when they both attended the Glasgow School of Art. Their work was shown at the eighth Vienna Secession Exhibition in 1900. Mackintosh's architectural career was a relatively short one, but of significant quality and impact. All his major commissions were between 1895 and 1906, including designs for private homes, commercial buildings, interior renovations and churches.

Unbuilt designs
Although moderately popular (for a period) in his native Scotland, most of Mackintosh's more ambitious designs were not built.

Designs for various buildings for the 1901 Glasgow International Exhibition were not constructed, neither was his "Haus eines Kunstfreundes" "Art Lovers house" of the same year. He competed in the 1903 design competition for Liverpool Cathedral, but failed to gain a place on the short-list (the winner was Giles Gilbert Scott).

Other unbuilt Mackintosh designs include:
- Railway Terminus
- Concert Hall
- Alternative Concert Hall
- Bar and Dining Room
- Exhibition Hall
- Science and Art Museum
- Chapter House

The House for An Art Lover (1901) was built in Bellahouston park, Glasgow after his death (1989–1996).

An Artist's Cottage and Studio (1901), known as The Artist's Cottage, was completed at Farr by Inverness in 1992. The architect was Robert Hamilton MacIntyre acting for Dr and Mrs Peter Tovell. Illustrations can be found on the RCAHMS Canmore site.

The first of the unexecuted *Gate Lodge, Auchinbothie (1901)* sketches was realised as a mirrored pair of gatehouses to either side of the Achnabechan and The Artist's Cottage drives, also at Farr by Inverness. Known as North house and South House, these were completed 1995-7.

MacKintosh died on December the 10th 1928 in London.

Andy Cameron

Andrew Graham Cameron MBE, was born on the 27th of June 1940, he is a Scottish comedian, television and radio broadcaster.

He was born in London while his father Hugh Cameron was serving in the British army during WW 2. Cameron was raised by his grandmother, Isabella "Bella" Cameron in the royal burgh of Rutherglen [which is a satellite suburb on the verge of Glasgow].Prior to becoming a comedian /TV presenter/radio broadcaster he had worked for a time with the Glasgow based structural engineering firm, Sir William Arrol & co and for Glasgow corporation transport.

He entered showbusiness when he was 32 years old, initially working in clubs. His act as a football hooligan led to him becoming a top comedy act in Scottish football clubs.

By Andy's own admission he was/is a Rangers fan who stood on the Ibrox slopes singing "the Sash" and other songs of that ilk but he is probably best known for writing and performing "Ally's Tartan army" for the Scottish National football team's appearance in the 1978 world cup. This song went to number 6 in the UK singles chart and led to two appearances for Andy on Top of the Pops in 1978.

Cameron promptly put all of the profits from this single hit into producing an album which he hoped to release while the world cup fever was still going strong in Scotland, he was too late-Scotland went out of the world cup early and his album fared equally badly.

Andy also released a song in the 1970's for his beloved Glasgow Rangers- "the Greatest team of all" which still appears on the odd Rangers compilation album. In

1975 he came second on New Faces leading to several performances on variety shows such as live at her Majesty's with Jimmy Tarbuck and "Tarby and friends"

In 1979, soon after the establishment of BBC Radio Scotland he was given a thirteen week contract to present a programme of music and humour. The show ran for eventually fifteen years.

He was voted radio personality of the year in 1984, he had his own series on BBC Scotland in 1979 and again in 1982. He was awarded Scottish television personality of the year for his 1983 series called "It's Andy Cameron"

In the early 1980's he was invited to speak in debates at Cambridge and Oxford universities alongside Arnold Brown and James Naughtie.

In 1984 Cameron presented STV's Hogmanay show. The following year he presented the BBC Scotland Hogmanay show and continued to do so until 1989.

His last Hogmanay appearance was in 1990in a short programme called "Andy's Scottish filling" which preceded the live BBC Hogmanay show.

In 1994 he joined the cast of "Take the high road" which was a TV soap. He played the part of a character called Chic Cherry until the last episode in 2003.

Cameron is a well known celebrity supporter of Rangers FC, in the early 1980's he caused some controversy by attacking the clubs anti-Catholic signing policy at an annual general meeting of the club.

He has a stand up act before Rangers home league matches.

In 1999 a follower of rival club Aberdeen FC ran from the away section at Ibrox to assault Cameron as he performed his routine prior to the kick off.

He currently works as an after dinner speaker. Furthermore he presented a show on "Clyde 2"On Sunday afternoons until the show ended in late 2009 when he was replaced by Tom Ferrie whose whose show is now networked by two or three other Scottish radio stations.

Cameron was appointed "Member of the Order of the British Empire" [MBE] in the 2015 New Year Honours for services to entertainment and charity in Glasgow.

Glen Daly

Born Bartholomew Francis McCann McGovern Dick he changed his name to Glen Daly for obvious reasons.

Daly was born in Glasgow where he attended St Marys school. On completing his education he started work in the Clydeside shipyards.

He began his stage career as a foil to Glasgow music hall artiste Lex McLean and his peers included Andy Stewart and the Alexander brothers.

The song that Glen is best known for is "The Celtic song" and it is still played at the home matches of Glasgow Celtic at Parkhead on match days.

I personally remember him as he lived only a street away from me in the old tenements at the boundary of Gorbals/Oatlands in the south side of Glasgow, although him and his wife Ella moved to Toryglen st in those lovely red-sandstone tenements at the far end of Oatlands [near to Richmond park].

Glen and his wife Ella [and son] lived at close number 3 in Toryglen st and 3 up on the top landing, he was often heard through his open tenement windae rehearsing his songs.

I actually attended the same primary school as Glen's son Terry Dick at the same time as he did, it was called St Bonaventure's primary school at the boundary line where Oatlands ended and the Gorbals began.

Daly also toured extensively and is probably best remembered for appearing on BBC Scotland show and The White Heather Club as well as many pantomimes at Glasgow's Pavilion theatre where he frequently topped the bill in variety shows.

Further afield from his native city Daly was also a popular performer at the Edinburgh Palladium and in Belfast.

He is also well remembered for being the resident host in the Ashfield club in the north of the city where did his one man show for many years and was given the nickname "Mr Glasgow" by many.
Daly can be heard on "Last FM". He has a Glasgow Celtic supports club named after him in Rothesay, Isle of Bute.

"The Celtic song" was featured in the US television programme "Lost"

Glen was born in Glasgow in 1920 and passed away in 1987.

Bill Tennent

Born in Rutherglen, he went to Glasgow High School before training as an actor at the Royal Scottish Academy of Music and Drama, where he was a contemporary of Andy Stewart and John Cairney.

When STV was being launched in 1957, he successfully auditioned and did not complete his course.

Scottish Television

One of his first jobs, apart from announcing, was as presenter of an advertising magazine, *Man About the House*. From there he went on to be anchorman on the news and current affairs programme, *Here and Now*.

He was involved in a wide range of television genres, including religion, education, documentaries, and reports from abroad.

Several chat shows were built around him, including *The Bill Tennent Show*, from the King's, Edinburgh, *Time Out with Tennent*, and *Time for Tennent*.

He presented of local and General Election programmes, and, as an outside broadcaster, was one of the ITV team at the wedding of Princess Alexandra and the Queen's jubilee celebrations. He also covered the opening of the Tay Road Bridge by the Queen Mother.
In the 1960s, he was the first recipient of the 'STV Personality of the Year' award.

Tributes

In an obituary in the *Glasgow Herald*, Bill Brown, then chairman of STV said: "In many respects, Bill was Mr STV during its first 20 years. He epitomised what the station was about. He was held in highest esteem by viewers, who regarded him as a personal friend."
David Johnstone, ex-director of programmes, who was director of most of the early Tennent shows, said: "He was a great television

professional, unflappable under pressure when everything was going out live."

Another former colleague said he was "always completely natural and unaffected."

When comedian Billy Connolly received a lifetime achievement award at the National Television Awards in January 2016 he remarked during his acceptance speech: "I'd like to thank Bill Tennant in Scotland, who was the first man to put me on television, and Michael Parkinson who was the first British man to put me on television."

After STV
When he left STV in the late 70s, it was to be mine host of the Marie Stuart Hotel, in Glasgow, which was sold in June 1992 when he decided to retire.

Death
Bill Tennent died at his Glasgow home in 1993, aged 59. He was survived by his wife, Margo, a daughter, Mandy, and son, Scott.

Authors note: As I have said before Rutherglen is one of the satellite suburban areas on the Glasgow fringe, so I have no problem including it in my book and I have the pleasure to say that I have visited Rutherglen on many occasions as a youth and later on in life when I come back hame to Glasgow for my annual holiday.

Chapter 10

Bits and Pieces

The cold winter of 1962/3

December 1962 gave parts of Scotland a white Christmas. Glasgow received its first snowfall on Christmas Day since in the post-war period. However, it was the early days of 1963 that were characterised by clear skies and plunging temperatures, with the coldest recorded temperature of -22.2°C logged in Braemar.

I clearly remember the winter of 62/63, I was a fourteen year old schoolboy in 62 and loved "having a go on the slides" in the streets of our housing scheme until some old lady would come out and sprinkle salt on the ice which would stop us wean having fun. We didn't realise at that early age how dangerous icy pavements could be for the elderly.

And into the new year there was no let up of the freezing conditions, it was so bad that for weeks on end all the football matches were postponed and a "Pools Panel" was set up to give "results" so people could still put their football coupons on every week.

These Arctic conditions were terrible and everyone called it "The Big Freeze". I started work as an apprentice bricklayer in April 1963 and I remember the men all telling me that they hadn't had a wage packet for three months after Christmas, they all had to sign on the dole.

Maggie McKay

Born in Glasgow in "61,never had a clue,
That the family I was living with was anything but true.

I knew my father loved me as indeed did all the rest,
but trying to get love from mum that proved to be a test.

Things happened now and then that made me stop and think,
do I really fit in here, sometimes my heart would sink.

Both grannies looked at me as if I had the plague,
I started asking questions but the answers they were vague.

Finally years later when the truth it did appear,
it all made so much sense to me and things became so clear.

My mother had abandoned me because she had no choice,
apparently back in those days young girls they had no voice.

My heart was deeply saddened when I sat there face to face
with the woman who had given me up because she fell from grace.

She doesn't feel the sadness that I did feel in my heart,
she went off to New Zealand and made a brand new start.

She thinks she did a good thing by leaving me behind,
I find it hard to swallow that she blocked me from her mind.

The siblings in this family were genuinely fine
but I always really felt that they weren't truly mine.

So I raise a toast to wee Andy Steedman, who's very deeply missed
for giving me the love and strength to feel I was truly blessed.

Authors note: This poem / story is a true account of a dear friend of
mine Maggie McKay.

Tradeston Tool store

I want to tell you a true story that happened to me when I was sixteen
years old. It was 1964 and I was a second year apprentice bricklayer
wanting to buy a new brick trowel for my work.

There was this great American brick-trowel called a "Marshalltown
trowel", so I walked into the Tradeston tool shop in Eglinton street in
the Gorbals and asked the shop assistant for one of these

"Marshalltown trowels". well he said to me that because of the American war in Vietnam all the metal in America was being used to make rifles but he could offer me another brick trowel which was just as good as a "Marshalltown trowel".

The assistant was so convincing that I bought this other trowel from him only to go over to Glasgow cross and look in another tool shop window display and it was full of these American "Marshalltown trowels".

I felt really let down that this guy from the Tradeston tool store could have told such a lie to a gullible 16 year old lad but it learnt me a lesson for later on in life. [but what a Riddy I got when I saw the other trowels.]

Housing schemes

In the1950s Glasgow city centre was divided into twenty-nine Comprehensive Development Areas, with much demolition and rebuilding proposed: two New Towns, East Kilbride and Cumbernauld, and expansive modern schemes were built on the outskirts of the city at Easterhouse, Drumchapel, Castlemilk and Pollok.

So where did you move to ? or did you stay in your tenement as it never got demolished?. Just after the end of WW2 Glasgow city planning department set out the future for New Towns and the housing schemes and also high rise flats [or multi storeys as we called them]. My family moved out to the new housing scheme of South Nitshill at the very end of 1960 when the back of our tenement collapsed. [which I will mention later.]

To me [and us] being brought up in the tenements was magic, you had all the shops you wanted and everyone knew each other and usually your Granda and Granny lived not far away. Then we were moved out to these new places, oh yes we had an inside toilet and a bath and a wee verandah but there wasn't the same soul and character in these new housing schemes that the old tenements had.

I just never "settled" in our housing scheme and kept going back at the weekends to see my wee Granny and my pals that we had left behind in the tenements. I don't know what the readers view is on this but I would rather have stayed in the tenements which was home to me.
Bus tokens

I remember years ago that there were these wee plastic tokens that you could use on the Glasgow corporation buses to pay your fare with. They were of different colours to denote their value. I'm sure that people who worked for Glasgow corporation got these every week with their pay-packet to pay for their transport getting to work.

It was only supposed to be corporation workers who were to get these but it seems everyone had them, sometimes you even got some of these tokens in your change from the shopkeeper. Do you remember?

Buchanan st Railway Station

Constructed in 1849 by the Caledonian Railway Company as its main terminus for the city, the original station buildings consisted of supposedly temporary wooden structures, which lasted until the 1930s. A goods station at the site opened in 1850. Services ran primarily northbound, to Aberdeen,Perth, and Stirling and other destinations.
The station was marked for closure and replacement in the "Bruce Report" about how to redevelop Glasgow in the post- Second World War period.
The plan included replacing Buchanan Street and Queen Street stations with a Glasgow North station on land including the site of Buchanan Street, but many times larger. There was also a similar scheme to replace Central and St Enoch stations with a Glasgow South station, but neither came to fruition.

This reprieve proved to be only temporary as the station was closed in 1966 as part of the rationalisation of the railway system devised by Richard Beeching, with most of its services running to Queen Street. The buildings were demolished in 1967. The 430 yd (390 m) Buchanan Street tunnel that ran from just out-with the station to Sighthill still exists, but public access is prohibited.

Glasgow Tobacco Lords

All around the city of modern-day Glasgow, street names serve as a reminder of its tobacco trade past. For example, in an area of down-town known as Merchant City, the Lords liked to flaunt their outlandish outfits and was the prime location where they chose to build their opulent mansions. Their own names as well as the names of their grand residences–and of the places that earned them their fortunes–still grace the streets of Glasgow today. The infamous Buchanan Street is named after Tobacco Lord Andrew Buchanan, while Virginia Street is named after Tobacco Lord Alexander Speirs' Virginia Mansion. His name was also given to Speirs Wharf. The same goes for Ingram Street and Dunlop Street, named after Archibald Ingram and James Dunlop. William Cunningham's over-the-top mansion on Queen Street still stands grand, and has been re-purposed as the Glasgow Gallery of Modern Art.

If the Tobacco Lords had their own style, their own streets and their own estates, then clearly they would have their own churches. The sensational St. Andrew's Parish Church, located near the home of Alexander Speirs, was commissioned by the Tobacco Lords as another way to showcase their fortunes. Still considered one of the most impressive 18th century churches in Scotland, St. Andrews is now a centre for performing art.

Authors note: It just shows you how we take for granted some of the street names in Glasgow without thinking of what the background behind them are related to

Saltcoats by the sea

How many of us went away for the Glasgow fair fortnight or a week down to Saltcoats for your summer holidays, it was great, the pure excitement of packing all the suitcases and getting ready to go over to the Toon and St Enoch's railway station to catch the steam engined train to Saltcoats. Then as the train pulled out of St Enoch's with the steam belching out of its funnel, you felt you were on top of the world. Your Da put all the suitcases on the overhead rack and you passed through the Gorbals with all its tenement buildings as you were on your way to the coast.

Then you arrived at Saltcoats railway station and immediately you could breathe in the sea-air, Oh what a feeling, then you walked to your wee place where you were going to stay for the next week or two.

As soon as you had unpacked you all went for a walk about the shops and took a wee walk along the shore, then us weans could play in the sand on the beach while your Da tried to set up the beach deck chairs for him and your Ma. Lots of folks would paddle in the water while throwing some salt water from the sea onto their face to try and get a sun tan. Sometimes your wee Granny came with you too.

The joy of being bought a pokey-hat ice cream cone and playing in the sand was pure magic and they even had their own wee "Shows" down there. Again us weans would be getting spoilt getting rides on the different things like the hobby horses and getting a stick of candy-floss and at night when you and the family went for a walk along the promenade you'd be looking at all the wee boats laying on their sides that the fishermen used and us weans playing on top of them.

It seemed every day the sun would shine [well maybe the odd wet day] and you made a bee-line to the beach after Ma had made the breakfast in the place you had rented.

It seems like half of Glasgow went to Saltcoats at the fair fortnight and my parents always bumped into someone they knew back in Glasgow.

Then at night time on the way back to your wee place your Ma or Da would buy you a poke of chips with plenty of salt and vinegar and this was pure dead magic. Then all of a sudden it was time to go back to Glasgow and you couldn't wait to tell your wee pals who unfortunately had no summer holiday about the great time you had. Your Ma always made sure that you brought back a stick of rock for those wee pals [remember it had Saltcoats printed all the way through it].

Oh what a great place for your summer holiday although some other people preferred going to Dunoon or Helensburgh, it was great going away but great to go back to your tenement and play all your games.

Old Phone boxes

Do you remember the old phone boxes in the streets with the A and B buttons, you put your 4 old pennies into the box then you dialled the number and if the person answered you pressed button A and you got connected and spoke to whoever you had called.

If you didn't get connected you pressed button B and your 4 pennies came down the wee chute back to you.

Of course some "bad boys" would shove pits of old newspaper up the B button chute to stop the 4 penny's from coming back to you. The person who "lost" their 4 pennies would storm off in "the huff" while the "bad boys" would see all this happening from afar and come and pull away the bit of newspaper, get the 4 penny's and off to the nearest shop to buy sweeties or a couple of "single fags".

A Glasgow joke

A Glasgow couple called Tam and Mary went on the Waverley paddle steamboat down the Clyde on a day trip down to the Ayrshire coast, as they left the Broomielaw this American tourist got talking to them and told them that his Grandparents had came from Glasgow.

He said he liked Glasgow but he was having difficulty trying to understand the "Glasgow slang". Anyway a few miles down the Clyde and Tam said to Mary "Ere, ere, ere, ere" and Mary said "Oh aye so it is".

The American shook his head in disbelief and said to Mary "I just heard your husband say "Ere, ere, ere, ere" and you said "so it is", can you translate please.

Mary turns round to the Yank and said "Nae problem" my husband Tam just said "There's Ayr over there.

Chapter 11

Miscellaneous

Miscellaneous

building with her twins' pram.

Families flee as wall collapses

TWENTY - three families hurriedly quit their homes in Fauldhouse Street, Oatlands, Glasgow, to-day when a large section of the outside fabric of the tenement collapsed into the backcourt.

Most of them grabbed a few possessions and shepherded their children away from the building where sinks and pipes had been left exposed.

Families with children sought shelter in the homes of friends.

CONDEMNED

The others stood in the street opposite their homes awaiting the Master of Works' decision on the property WHICH WAS CONDEMNED BEFORE THE WAR.

Then word came through—no one would be allowed to return to their home. The property WAS REPAIRABLE, but the cost

would be so high the corporation would have to decide whether to repair it or pull it down.

In the meantime, the families would have to make their own arrangements for alternative accommodation.

If the corporation decided not to repair the property they could apply for new homes on hardship grounds.

But after a further inspection it was decided to shore up the damaged wall immediately, and it is hoped that this will be completed by to-night and that nearly all the families will then be allowed to return to their homes.

A man whose home was among the most seriously affected was at work unaware of what had happened.

"LIKE EXPLOSION".

He is Mr Thomas Gillan, who left shortly after seven o'clock for his work as a builder at Castlemilk.

One of his neighbours, Mr Michael

McAleavy (44), a labourer, who lives on the ground floor of the next close, No. 32, said — "It sounded like an explosion. I thought the whole building was coming down."

One of the first to leave the building was Mr John Potts (35), a Cleansing Department worker, who had just finished the night shift.

"There was a rumble and my 11-year-old son Robert said 'The chimney has fallen down.'

"But when we looked into the backcourt and saw the tons of rubble and clouds of dust we decided to get out immediately."

Mr Potts, his wife, Alice, and other members of their family, 11-month-old John and seven-year-old Alister went to a neighbour's house.

REFUGE . . .

Most of the displaced families found refuge in the homes of relatives and friends, but not them all.

Standing shivering in the street, Mrs Annie Hendry (37), who lives on a first-floor house at 32 Fauldhouse Street, said—"I don't know where to go or what to do. I have sent three of my children to school and taken the other two to my mother-in-law's round the corner, but we can't stay there because there's no room."

claim by painter who lost leg

Colvilles, he says, failed in their duty to take reasonable care for his safety.

BLOOD TRANSFUSION

This was the headlines in the Evening Times newspaper in Glasgow on December 13th 1960, this was when the back of my old tenement in Oatlands collapsed, due to lack of maintenance and also subsidence. I had came back from Holyrood school that day, walking all the way from Aitkenhead rd [where the annexe of Holyrood was situated] through Polmadie and into my tenement which had Police and fire-brigade officers working underneath arc floodlights to try and see if they could prop up the back elevation of our tenement.

What a shock !!! some of the families including mine were allowed to stay in our house while others were not as their part was too dangerous. I was only a few weeks from my 13th birthday and this day has always

158

remained with me as one of the worst days of my life. My parents were told by Glasgow corporation that they would be given the choice of 3 new housing schemes and my Da and Ma chose the first one which was out at South Nitshill [Pollok direction]. I hated leaving the soo-side behind where we had all the shops, picture houses, barber shops etc that we needed.

Oh and what a shock moving out to this South Nitshill housing scheme which was about 7 miles away from the Toon. This new housing scheme only had a couple of shops and we had to walk half a mile to Nitshill village for the fish and chip shop, hairdressers, bookies and pubs. Even today as I write my book I still feel "Cheated" of having to leave the soo-side behind.

I did leave Glasgow when I was 20 years old to start on my travels of building bricks which took me to countries halfway round the world but Oh what I would have given just to have spent those years between the ages of 13 and 20 to remain in my old tenement where we had that great close knit community spirit. Yes even today as a 71 year old man I still feel "cheated" of those 7 years.

This wonderful poem / story was by "Avril's Mother" circa 1920/30

I was born in Possilpark
And see no reason to keep it dark

'Twas a clean and friendly place with little strife
Where we helped one another to cope with life

A 'close' knit community we were In fact
And tried to keep the clan intact

Whenever a house 'to let' was sighted
Somebody's nuptials were expedited

It was usual to have an aunt next door
And a brother and sister on another floor

We had no electricity - nothing but gas
Some had pianos - a touch of class!

Others, the charm of music conceding
Just kept canaries with an air of breeding

Street games were rounders and smuggleerie
Leap frog, marbles or spinning a peerie

Ba', beds, kick the bucket, sometimes peever
Alas! they've disappeared – like scarlet fever

Flocks of sheep went to market with dog and drover
On streets where 'tis dangerous now to cross over

In Bardowie Street, Granny Hope kept hens
And Flannigan's Farm had pigs in pens

Horse drawn water carts would spray
The dusty streets on a summer's day

While bare foot weans with shouts of laughter
Were drenched to the skin as they followed after

Whether the weather was sunny or rainy
There was plenty of fun around 'Staunalaney'

The building that stood in grand isolation
Across from the church where the congregation

On Sabbath days by the bells were summoned
To remember god – nor forget Henry Drummond!

His sermons were classics, never trifles
(Oh, the Boy's Brigade drilled in the street with rifles)

The park stretched over to Keppochhill
We sledged there in winter with many a spill

Or climbed Sparrows Dyke bounding Craigbank Gardens
Where now St. Theresa's dispenses pardons

Here one thing simply must be said
None of US would have knocked off her head!

We knew something of God but little of schism
At school we learned the catechism

The ten commandments we knew by heart
And tried to keep them – at least in part!

It did us no harm to keep these laws
Since we hadn't been told what a complex was!

Teachers were held in awe of affection
As they used, or did not use, the tawse for correction

They taught us much more than the basic three R's
And inspired us to hitch our wagons to stars

All the shopkeepers were personal friends
(Except the co-op with its dividends)

They supplied all our needs from jam to jotters
And we went to school with their sons and daughters

There was Jimmy and Davie and Willie and Sammy
And several shops run by somebody's granny

Mrs McCormack took clothes to be mangled
In her shop where a cage with a green parrot dangled

She sold broken biscuits – a farthing a poke
Plus free entertainment when the parrot spoke

161

Old Granny Dearie across the street
Made marvellous balls, our favourite sweet

You could make one last – an acquired skill -
While you walked from Possil right to Lambhill

The Chemist's stock was arrayed on a shelf
The various ingredients he mixed himself

Syrup of squills, glycerine, ipecachuana wine
Threepence worth of this and your chest was fine

Parma Violets, Jockey Club, Ashes of Roses
Were perfumes dispensed in twopenny doses

Possilpark had a host of great personalities
Worthy to grace more prestigious localities
But such is progress and march of time
We sink to ridiculous from the sublime

Whereas we were people of worthy and variety
Now, an impersonal heartless society

Has levelled us all – hero, genius and mystic –
To the common ground of a state statistic

One might go on talking thus 'Off the Cuff'
But however nostalgic 'enough is enough!

Half-time Scores

Years ago when I started going to watch football matches way back in
the mid-1950's us weans used to always get a "lift over" the turnstile
by one of the men who paid his entrance fee and "pretended" the boy

he was "lifting over" was his son. A big thanks from me to all the men who gave me a lift over when I was a wean.

Back in those far off days you had guys walking round beside the pitch selling peanuts and macaroon bars it was always a great exciting day and when your team ran out it gave you butterflies in your stomach.

Money was tight back in those days but I always remember the match programme being on sale for 3-d old money, it gave you the names of all the players in the teams that day [no substitutes back then] just 11 players a side.

Although I have to say what amazed me was in the match programme you had letters A,B C.D etc and say A would represent Aberdeen and B was Dundee, because what you had in every football park was a big board and at half-time you would look at it and it would say A 2-0 or B 0-1. So at half time this meant that Aberdeen [A] the home team were winning 2-0 at half time and Dundee [B] the home team were getting beat 0-1.

Seems funny nowadays with all the smart phones we have when we can get instant results about the other team's scores any time we want. Just shows you how far we have came eh.

Then when the match was over you couldn't wait to buy the Pink evening Times or the Green Citizen newspapers to find out all the final football results.

And also today you can place a bet on a football match from your mobile phone, changed days indeed from when I was a young man !!

GANG WAR IN CASTLEMILK

Rival gangs from Rutherglen, Castlemilk and Glasgow clashed in Castlemilk late on Sunday night.

About 60 youths gathered at the corner of Barlia Drive and Castlemilk Drive.

When police swooped on the crowd, the gangs scattered but it is understood a number of arrests were made.

The accused appeared at Govan Police Court on Monday charged with forming part of a disorderly crowd.

No plea was taken and they were remitted to the Sheriff Court and ordered to be detained for further enquiries.

Since the scheme went up nine years ago a number of similar incidents have been reported.

Most people are under the impression that Castlemilk has cut-throats and neds walking the streets, while in fact the place is just like any other new housing scheme.

Usually the people concerned in these fights don't even live in Castlemilk and it's no wonder that the scheme gets a bad name.

Full credit and thanks to the Castlemilk local History Group.

Chapter 12

Topics

Topics

Glasgow Botanic Gardens is a botanical garden located in the West end of Glasgow, Scotland. It features several glasshouses, the most notable of which is the Kibble Palace.

The Gardens has a wide variety of temporate and tropical flora, aherb garden, a chronological bed with plants arranged according to their introduction to Scotland, the UK's national collection of tree ferns and a world rose garden officially opened in 2003 by Princess Tomohito of Mikasa.

The river Kelvin runs along the north side of the Gardens and continues through the Kelvingrove park, the Kelvin walkway providing an uninterrupted walking route between the two green spaces.

The Botanic Gardens was awarded a Green flag Award in 2011.

In 1817 about 8 acres (32,000 m²) of land were laid out at Sandyford, near Sauchiehall Street, Glasgow, and run by the Royal Botanic Institution of Glasgow (founded by Thomas Hopkirk of Dalbeth), and were intended to supply the University of Glasgow. William Hooker was regius professor botany at Glasgow University, and contributed to the development of the Botanic Gardens before his appointment to the directorship of Kew Gardens in London.

The Gardens moved to its current location in 1842. The gardens were originally used for concerts and other events, and in 1891 the gardens were incorporated into the Parks and Gardens of the City of Glasgow.

The site was once served by a railway line, and Botanic Gardens Railway station remains today in a derelict state as a remarkable example of a disused station.

It is hidden behind some trees and a metal fence blocks access to the platforms. Kirklee railway station also lies just inside the gardens.

The Kibble Palace is a 19th-centurywrought iron framed glasshouse, covering 2137 m². Originally designed for John Kibble by architects James Boucher and James Cousland for his home at Coulport on Loch Long in the 1860s, the components were cast by Walter MacFarlane at his Saracen foundry in Possilpark. Eventually brought up the River Clyde by barge to the Botanic Gardens, it was fully erected at its current location in 1873 by Boyd of Paisley.

The building structure is of curved wrought iron and glass supported by cast iron beams resting on ornate columns, surmounted on masonry foundations. It was initially used as an exhibition and concert venue, before being used for growing plants from the 1880s. Benjamin Disraeli and William Ewart Gladstone were both installed as Rectors of the University of Glasgow in the palace, in 1873 and 1879 respectively - its last use as a public events venue, before becoming wholly used for the cultivation of temperate plants.

The main plant group is the collection of New Zealand and Australian tree ferns, some of which have lived here for 120 years and which now form the national tree fern collection.

In the 1920s a statue was added in the palace to "King Robert of Sicily" a figure from the works of Longfellow.

This is by the Scottish sculptor George Henry Paulin.

In 2004 a £7 million restoration programme was initiated to repair corrosion of the ironwork. The restoration involved the complete dismantling of the Palace, and the removal of the parts to Shepley engineers Shafton works, South Yorkshire for specialised repair and conservation.

The plant collection was removed completely for the first time ever and the ironwork was rebuilt over a rearranged floor-plan, giving the Palace a prolonged life. It re-opened to the public in November 2006.

The building contains a large collection of orchids, carnivorous plants and tree ferns.

The Glasgow Subway

The **Glasgow Subway** is an underground rapid transit line in Glasgow, Scotland. Opened on 14 December 1896, it is the third-oldest underground metro system in the world after the London Underground and the Budapest Metro It is also one of the very few railways in the world with a track running gauge of 4 ft (1,219 mm). Formerly a cable railway, the Subway was later electrified, but its twin circular lines were never expanded. The line was originally known as the **Glasgow District Subway**, but was later renamed Glasgow Subway Railway. It was so called when taken over by the Glasgow Corporation who renamed it the **Glasgow Underground** in 1936. Despite this Rebranding, many Glaswegians continued to refer to the network as "the Subway". In 2003 the name "Subway" was officially readopted by its operator, the Strathclyde Partnership for Transport (SPT). A £40,000 study examining the feasibility of an expansion into the city's south side was conducted in 2005 while a further commitment from Labour in 2007 to extend to the East End was also to no avail.

The route is a loop almost 6.5 miles (10.5 km) long and extends both north and south of the River Clyde. The tracks have the unusual narrow gauge of 4 ft (1,219 mm), and a nominal tunnel diameter of 11 feet (3.35 m), even smaller than that of the deep-level lines of the London Underground (11 feet 8 ¼ inches or 3.56 metres at their smallest); the rolling stock is considerably smaller.

The system is described as two lines, the Outer Circle and Inner Circle, but this simply refers to the double track, having trains running clockwise and anticlockwise respectively around the same route although in separate tunnels. Stations use a variety of platform layouts including single island platforms, opposing side platforms and in some stations such as Hillhead one side and one island platform.

The subway's running lines are entirely underground, but the maintenance depot at Broomloan Road (located between the Govan and Ibrox stations) is above ground, as was the earlier depot, also at Govan. Prior to modernisation, trains used to be hoisted by crane onto and off the tracks. Modernisation brought the installation of points and a ramp between Govan and Ibrox where trains can exit the tunnel system to terminate for engineering, cleaning or storage.

The system is owned and operated by the Strathclyde Partnership for Transport (SPT), formerly Strathclyde Passenger Transport, and carried 13.16 million passengers in the period 2005–06. The Subway has been policed by British transport Police since 2007.

The system is not the oldest underground railway in Glasgow: that distinction belongs to a 3.1 mi (5.0 km) section of the Glasgow City and District Railway opened in 1863, now part of the North Clyde Line of the suburban railway network, which runs in a sub-surface tunnel under the city centre between High Street and west of Charing cross. Another major section of underground suburban railway line in Glasgow is the Argyle Line, which was formerly part of the Glasgow Central Railway.

The Subway runs from 06:30 to 23:40 Monday to Saturday and 10:00 to 18:12 on Sunday.

Taggart

The Scottish BAFTA-winning pilot episode, "Killer", directed by Laurence Moody and broadcast in 1983, introduced the character Detective Chief Inspector (DCI) Jim Taggart (played by Mark McManus until his death in 1994), a tough and experienced detective who had worked his way up through the ranks. His original sidekick was detective Sergeant (DS) Peter Livingstone (Neil Duncan). Livingstone represented the new breed of young graduates entering the police force, and frequently had a difficult relationship with Taggart as a result. Taggart's boss in the pilot was Superintendent Robert Murray (Tom Watson), known as "The Mint" after the well-known sweet. This humour was continued in the subsequent series, when Taggart's boss after the second episode ("Dead Ringer") being Superintendent Jack McVitie (Iain Anders), nicknamed "The Biscuit" because he shared his name with a popular brand of biscuits. Another important character was Taggart's wife Jean (Harriet Buchan), whose physical disability (she was a wheelchair user) did not prevent her from pursuing a number of interests in life while her cynical husband stuck mainly to his job. Throughout the McManus era, there was nearly always a sub-plot in every episode which involved the domestic life of the Taggarts which, on occasion, became intertwined with the case being investigated.

The most memorable of these was the Taggart's ongoing care of Jean's senile Aunt Hettie (Sheila Donald), whom Jim despises and begrudges staying in his house. This sub-plot ran through 1990-91, until the Hettie character was finally killed off in the 1991 season finale ("Violent Delights").

In 1987 the character of Mike Jardine [James McPherson] was introduced, Neil Duncan also left the series in 1987 and in 1990 a new female sidekick, Jackie Reid (Blythe Duff), was introduced.

McManus died in 1994, during the filming of an episode. Taggart's absence in the broadcast story was explained by his being in meetings with the Chief Constable throughout. In 1995 the episode "Black Orchid" opened with Taggart's funeral. Despite the death of the title character, the series went unchanged. Jardine was promoted to Detective Inspector and DC Stuart Fraser (Colin McCredie) was introduced, becoming the long-suffering sidekick to Jardine, former long-suffering sidekick to Taggart. Fraser was later revealed to be gay. (McCredie had made an early appearance in Taggart when he played a suspect part of a youth gang). DI Robbie Ross (John Michie) joined the team in 1998 (Michie had made an early appearance in *Taggart* in 1990, when he played a suspect called Robby Meiklejohn in an episode called "Love Knot"). When MacPherson left the series in 2002 his character was killed off and replaced with DCI Matt Burke, formerly of Special Branch (played by Alex Norton, who had previously appeared in the series playing murder suspect George Bryce in 1986, in the episode "Knife Edge").

Much was made of the platonic relationship between Jardine and Reid. The two were shown to share a brother/sister-like bond. Both pursued a number of relationships with other characters over the years. Reid even got married, but later separated from her husband, who then died. The personal relationships of the police officers in this series were shown as nothing to be envious of: Reid once described herself, Burke, Ross and Fraser as three divorcees and a celibate homosexual (in the episode "Penthouse and Pavement"). After filming was completed on series 26, in December 2009, Colin McCredie was informed that he and his character would not be returning for filming of the next series.

Authors note: I don't know about you but I always felt that Mike Jardine [James McPherson] was too young to take over from Jim Taggart [Mark McManus]. I'm not doubting Mcpherson's acting ability at all as I think he is a fine actor but I think the role should have been given to someone in the same ilk as Detective Chief Inspector Matt Burke [Alex Norton] whom I think played the part brilliantly. Of course you may not agree but that's just my line of thinking. Although I still watch Taggart repeats on free-view TV avidly. Such a shame Mark McManus died.

The Great Storm of 1968

The 1968 Hurricane was a deadly storm that moved through the central belt of Scotland during mid-January 1968. It was described as central Scotland's worst natural disaster since records began and the worst gale in the United Kingdom.

Some said that the damage resembled what happened during the Clydebank Blitz in 1941.

20 people died from the storm, with 9 dead in Glasgow. 700 were left homeless, such high wind speeds in an urban area were equivalent to those witnessed in Paris during cyclone Lothar in 1999.

The origins of this violent storm appear to be from a cold front near Bermuda on 13th of January 1968. The system moved north of the Azores the next day and still appeared as a shallow low pressure area. In the next 24 hours, this low explosively deepened 50 millibars to 956mb and passed over central Scotland. The storm continued to move over northern Europe before dissipating on 18th of January 1968.

15th of January began as a mild day, then temperatures grew cooler as the day progressed before the great storm happened. In Glasgow alone, over 300 houses were destroyed and 70.000 homes were damaged. Due to the strong winds, half of Glasgow's council homes were damaged.

Many people evacuated the then Europe's tallest flats as they began swaying. Officials said at least seven ships sank or went adrift in the river Clyde causing hundreds of thousands of pounds damage. A Glasgow police spokesman said that it was "absolute havoc" in the city, electrical power also failed in Glasgow, leaving the whole city in darkness.

After the storm moved away, the death toll continued to rise. 30 people died from repairing houses. On 16th of January 1968 about 150 troops from Edinburgh came to Glasgow to help with the clean-up operation. There was little national press coverage of the storm, despite it affecting most of Northern England, North of Ireland and Scotland. An interest free loan of £500.000 was given by the Labour government to the affected areas. Singer Frankie Vaughan began to raise funds for the victims of the storm by holding special concerts at the Alhambra Theatre in Glasgow.

After the devastation of the storm in the area Glasgow city council quickly imposed a new policy to improve housing in the city.

On a personal note I was a 5th year apprentice bricklayer working out at Bridge O' Weir, we were building private houses and when we arrived on the site the next day there were brick walls blown down all over the place which we had to rebuild, the firm I served my apprenticeship with was John Dickie and sons and they said that their insurance policy covered all the destruction.

Midgie Rakin

Well how many of us done it? I was one of them and loved the thrill of trying to look for a find a "luxy". Of course we would be on the look-out for Ginger bottles that people had thrown into the open middens because at that time [the 1950's for me] there was a penny or two deposit on them and if you found one, you couldn't run fast enough to the nearest shop to get the penny or two deposit money so you could buy some sweeties.

Although some shopkeepers said that bottle never came from my shop, so you had to keep going to find a shop that would accept them and give you your sweetie money.

Lots of times you didn't do "midgie rakin" in your own back court but went further afield to other tenements and this was all part of the adventure to us weans. You might come across a toy that was thrown out into the auld midden bin but to you it looked perfect.

Some days in the school summer holidays you spent the whole day midgie rakin going from one back court to another. Then when you found a "luxy" you'd shout out Aw look what I've found and immediately the shout went up [I'm baggin Hawfwers] from your pals, that was the unwritten law of the "Midgie rakers".

At the end of the day if you had found a toy that looked in good order you could actually sell it for a penny to some wean who liked the toy and more importantly who had a penny or two to spare.

Then when you eventually went hame for your tea and your Ma would be screaming at you "You been midgie rakin again hivin't ye" and you always answered "Naw no me Ma" then she said "well how come your covered fae heid tae toe in ashes"!!!!!

Of course that wouldn't happen today as "health and safety" would go bananas but it never did us weans any harm did it? and nowadays how could you "midgie rake" a Wheelie bin anyway eh.

I look back now on those days and didn't we truly have a wonderful childhood growing up in the tenements, no computer games for us or videos, just playing our own games in the streets under the watchful eyes of our Granny's or Ma's or neighbours who were doing their windae hingin". I honestly feel sorry for the weans of today who will never experience all the games and adventure that us weans of that era had.

The Steamie

Nowadays most of us have washing machines in our kitchens or utility rooms but for our Ma's and Granny's years ago it was a different story for them.

They would have paid in advance for their weekly slot at the Steamie nearest to them, or to give it its official name "The Washhouse". first of all the clothing and bed-sheets etc was piled into a pram and then your Ma or Granny "bumped" the pram down the tenement stair and then pushed it along the street until they reached the Steamie.

Then they would sweat hard for a few hours doing their washing and then trying to get them dried before placing them back in their pram and pushing it all along the street until they came to their tenement close-mouth and proceeded to "bump" the pram back up the stair till they reached their door and put all the newly washed clothes into the drawers or cupboards/wardrobes.

Then sat down to have a well earned cup of tea. Of course while they were in the Steamie they got talking to the other women there and lots of news [or gossip] was exchanged and if anyone had been up to no good then their ears must have been burning as that person became "The talk of the Steamie".

There was another service that the Steamie offered and that was a hot bath and for threepence [or was it sixpence, I can't remember] you had the luxury of having a hot bath. In the tenements most of us never had inside bathrooms with a bath or even an inside toilet!!

You would climb up the stairs in the Steamie and sit on a bench waiting your call while the attendant filled your bath up with hot water using a "turn-key" from outside of your bath cubicle. When you lowered yourself into the bath [usually the water was red-hot] the attendant from outside your cubicle shouted more hot or cold water, you always shouted more cold but just as you were getting used to the heat of the water and using the carbolic soap given by the office down below where you also got your towel from, the attendant banged on your door "time up". You then stood on a wooden duck board and dried yourself. Oh How you felt great and actually felt six-feet tall !!. Yes today we think nothing of waking up in the morning and having a hot shower or bath in out homes then chucking your clothes in the washing machine but oh how it was different for out Ma's, Granny's and Great Granny's back then.

Chapter 13

Peoples stories

Danny Gill

I was born In the southern general hospital on 11th of January 1948 to my loving parents Daniel and Martha with my sister big Jeanette being 4 years older, my Ma and Da left their house in Snowdon st in the Hutchensontown part of the Gorbals and moved to 40 Fauldhouse st in   Oatlands which some called the "up-market" area of the Gorbals.

I had a wonderful time growing up as a wean in the soo-side, attending St Bonaventure's primary school, then St Bonaventure's junior secondary for 1 year before moving onto Holyrood senior secondary because I was top of the class with top marks in all my exams. Although I must say I never liked school and always feel "Hemmed In" I wanted to be free of sitting in a classroom and always had this wanderlust in me which I acted on in my working life to come.

I came back for my school one day and the back of our tenement had collapsed [of which I have already mentioned previously in my miscellaneous chapter of this book], I was only a few weeks off of my 13th birthday and we were shipped out to the new housing scheme of South Nitshill which I never really settled in and always felt a part of me was torn-apart having to leave the soo-side.

Anyway I left school at 15 years of age, with no qualifications and remember when the bell sounded on my last day at Holyrood school I ran out of the gate and threw my school bag up in the air shouting out "I'm free".

I started work as an apprentice bricklayer and completed my 5 year apprenticeship with a firm called John Dickie and sons and they and the bricklayers there taught me my trade well, which would take me halfway round the world.

As I said I always had this wanderlust in me and after my apprenticeship was completed, I stayed in Glasgow for 6 months then one Friday I jacked in the building site I was working on and said to myself right Danny son I'm off to London.

I had always been told by the older bricklayers in Glasgow that London was a great town for bricklayers with tons of work there.

I got the train to London and and got off at Euston railway station at 7 am on a Sunday morning without knowing anyone there, of course my first job was to get digs, I did but it was like a hostel place and I never liked it that much. but you have to start somewhere don't you.

Next morning I bought the evening news newspaper and looked for the building trade jobs section. I was amazed there was over 80 jobs for bricklayers, I phoned up the first one and started work at 8 am the next morning. All went well and was getting paid £4-10/- per day [wasn't too bad for 1968, not great but not bad]. I stayed with this sub-contractor for a few months then I saw other sub-contractors were paying £6 per shift so Danny boy was on the move again.

I stayed in London for about 6 months then I got a wee bit home-sick so went back to Glasgow and worked there for about 4 months but the wanderlust was biting me again, so it was tool bag, bead [level] and suitcase and back to London and started work again and the money was going up all the time , it was just a matter of looking in the newspaper to see who was paying the most.

I had many friends by this time round the Elephant & Castle are of south London, met quite a few other Glaswegians and used to have a great drink with them at the weekends, then I met this London girl called Maggie who was 18 years older than me but was a good looker and cut a long story short we started living together [yes living in sin !!].

Life for me was brilliant in London, I was living with Maggie, had plenty of pals, getting paid good money, but even though living in London I still liked to travel and ended up working in North, South, East and West London. I would travel back to Glasgow about once every three months to see my Ma and Da and watch my team Celtic play.

178

I had been in London almost 6 years when Maggie and me split up, I had plenty of money saved up so I went back to Glasgow for an extended holiday and it was there one day I was walking along Argyle st when I said to myself right I'm going to Australia and I did.

I landed in Australia in 1974 after paying for a one way aeroplane ticket to Sydney, I was always told the Oz was the land of sunshine and opportunity, so I gave myself 2 weeks to find out the "lay of the land". I was living in a hotel in the Kings cross area of Sydney which was then the red light district!! I asked Kelly the Australian barman what newspaper do you but for building trade workers.

He laughed at me and said I thought you were here just for a holiday, he said don't you know Australia is going through a bed recession? **Aw naw** I had about £100 left and right away left the hotel I was staying in and moved into the pub where Kelly the barman worked as it was a lot cheaper. Anyway I was getting worried as my money was going fast but I eventually got a start as a bricklayer and was getting good money [$50 per shift]. I had been working for about 3 months and saved a fair bit of money up and things were looking good until I met this New Zealand girl and things took a turn for the worse. We eventually moved down to Melbourne after me living in Sydney for a year but that was a complete disaster and Trudy my New Zealand girlfriend and me split up [[its a long story but that and other parts of my life are told in my autobiography = "Have Trowel Will Travel"]] anyway I stayed in Melbourne for a year but after two years of living and working in Oz the wanderlust bit me again and I found myself living and working back again In London and believe it or not moving back in with Maggie again.

After 6 months the wanderlust bit again and I found myself working in West Germany [with a stop over in Belgium first of all] for about 9 months, then back to London to live and bricklaying again then another 6 months went by and I found myself working back in West Germany again, [with a stop over in Holland this time] it was just like the TV show Auf Wiedersehen pet and I found myself playing the part of Dennis as there were 30 of us from the UK and I was the only

179

one who spoke or read German so I was the shop-steward. After about 4 months it was tool bag and level and back on the 'plane to London.

I then started drinking in a pub near to Waterloo railway station where I met my wife to be Maureen [or Mo as she was called] we had 3 daughters but unfortunately Mo and me split up but I always went back every Friday night and gave money from my wages to Mo for our girls and I would always take them out and make sure they had clothes etc and we never lost our bond between Father and daughters and we still meet regularly to this day, they were all born in the London area and only a fairly short distance from where I live now.

Back to me working in London again I was working on building sites all over the London area and started becoming foreman bricklayer on different sites. Then the wanderlust bit me and I was off to Dublin to live and work, Ireland is my ancestral home as my Da's Mother and Father both came from Donegal and I remember them clearly when I was a wean. After a while in Dublin building bricks/blocks and drinking the black coffee [Guinness]. Back to London and building bricks again but the years were flying in and I was 40 years old.

My love life wasn't as good as it was when I was in my 20's but I still had the odd fling now and again. Then disaster my Da who had been diagnosed as having Alzheimers disease died and I flew back up to Glasgow to lay my Da to rest God Bless him , he never drank or smoked in his life, just a pure honest hard worker. So Now I reach the age of 50 and the wanderlust bit me again and I found myself travelling over to Belfast and started working on the new Belfast Hilton at the Markets area of the town. I was there for about 6 months then found myself down in Dublin again, working in Dublin and then out in County Kildare. I was in Ireland for about eighteen months this time and met a lot of good mates but all those heavy concrete blocks took their toll on my, see I was mainly used to building face bricks. It was while I was in Dublin that Tracy my eldest daughter got married so I flew back to London to give her away and walked her down the aisle. Although I went back to Dublin I was only there about another 3 months and I flew back to London once again to live and work.

So now I am in my mid-50's and the work for bricklayers that I though would always be there had dried up and I found myself having to sign on the dole !!.

After a year or so this recession lifted and I found myself working as foreman bricklayer again. One of my other Daughters Susan got married and I proudly gave her away too.

All of a sudden I'm 60 years old and it looks like another recession is on the way and I'm starting to suffer from arthritis and wear and tear of working in the building trade for over 45 years.

My daughters have had children so now I'm a Granda and it's a great feeling.

I just turn 61 years old and the recession had hit hard and actually this was the end of my working career although I didn't realise it at the time.

I was living in a room in a pub at New Cross in south London called the 5 Bells and my room was at the very top of the stairs and it was so sore on my knees with my arthritis and I was suffering from slight heart trouble so I applied for sheltered housing accommodation and because of my medical condition got it within 3 weeks of applying. So that's me now living in sheltered housing at the age of 71 but what a wonderful Life that I have lived.

My youngest daughter Danielle and her Partner Mitch have two sons Bobby and Freddy and along with my Tracy+Mark who have Amber and Sonny and Susan + Paul who have Chloe, Phoebe and Elsie, that makes me a Granda 7 times over. Life is so good and I have so much to be thankful for.

This was just a short summarised account of my life otherwise to tell my life story would have taken all of the book up !! but I did write my autobiography as I mentioned before its called "Have Trowel Will Travel" which obviously goes into my life in detail.

Geraldine Baird

I grew up in Hamilton Road Rutherglen in 1950. I was the youngest of three sisters and it has to be said I was 'spoilt rotten'. I was told I looked like one of those scraps, the ones of an angel on a puffy white cloud, a wee cherub with nut brown curly hair, just sitting with her arms crossed smiling sweetly.

My Father was a Navvy and he worked in the Steel works at Clyde-bridge, he was a powerful man and would cycle home from working on the 'slag' for ten hours with his simmet soaked in sweat. He had been reared on a farm in Derry and knew hard work all his life. Hired out for ten bob when he was nine and could work a brace of horses and plough from that tender age. Working all over his Townland he sometimes landed in a good farm with kind folk and sometimes not, hunger was never far away. He was the oldest of 12 and handed in his earnings to his Mother who was badly in need of them.

My Mother's family were from Keady in county Armagh in Ireland and hers was a very different upbringing, they knew no want and she was a bookish woman who loved reading, loved Ireland, was fiercely Republican and immersed herself in Irish Culture.

We were raised then in a political and cultural Irish family the only difference being we lived in Scotland, I was 'culturally schizophrenic'.

Every Sunday I was taken to the Gorbals Church Hall [actually it was the old Synagogue in South Portland st in the Gorbals area]to learn my 'steps' from Charlie Kelly.

God knows his heart must have been roasted as I clomped about trying to remember one two three four five six seven and hop skip.... To be fair it did keep me in good stead for the hundreds of Ceilis I went to when I was older, I loved the Grand March Charlie never taught us that one!

On a Sunday we would sit in the 'front room' and listen to 78's [old records before the 45 rpm came into fashion] my Father had bought at the Barras, Bridie Gallacher, Father Sydney MacEwan and later on when the radiogram was adapted for LPs my Mother would play Paddy Tunney, Seamus Ennis, and always Wullie Brady, Dominic Behan and Republican songs like Boolavogue, 'All around me hat', The Croppy Boy, etc, so at school when we were asked to sing our 'party piece' for the Christmas Party mine was 'The Foggy Dew' not the most popular rendition that afternoon!!

We lived in a two room and kitchen with inside bathroom and I never felt 'poor' I never once heard my parents talk about money and yet it must have been tight. My Father worked 'doublers' and did joinery and building work on the side, every penny came into the house.

My Mother was determined that us 3 girls would get a good education. When she was young she worked in Bridgeton as a Doctors Dispenser and I think she saw a lot of downtrodden, poor women with no choice but to depend on their husbands, often they did not get much of the man's earnings to feed and clothe the family.

Of course times were different, women had fewer choices but by God Kate's girls would have all the choices which were available.

The result was the three of us were sent to a Franciscan Convent Fee Paying School in Bothwell.

I don't know how she did it, not just the fees but the travel and the uniforms, expensive panama hats and blazers from Paisleys clothes shop.

I stayed there till I was a teenager and my Mother's hopes were fulfilled as each of us went to University and we were indeed economically independent.

Growing up in our home gave me a blueprint for later life, a moral compass and a very loud voice to get my parents attention.

Also my love of reading and of Ireland and my faith, they all come from the start I was given by my parents and my wider family. We were immigrants and had to 'stick together' we helped each other and gave back to the community, family was all but everyone else had to be considered and helped if needed.

I had the best of it, the NHS, free education, growing up in an innocent time. and later on being able to be involved in CND, Hippie-dom and living in a time when men went to the moon and women began to strive for equality.

I was so Blessed .... God bless you Kate and Paddy and thank you bringing me into the world, I miss you still.

Authors note: Charlie Kelly who taught Geraldine Irish dancing died at an early age, he was only 49 years old when he passed away. He taught Irish dancing in several halls in the Gorbals area and Kinning park etc. He was sadly missed by everyone in the Irish community in Glasgow and further afield.

Liz Armour Crosbie

Growing up in Govanhill

My whole childhood was spent growing up in Govanhill born in Batson street with my six sisters and one brother in our two bedroom flat we were close not that wee had a choice with having to share everything but it's made us all still very close to this day.

I went to Victoria primary which was on my street where I lived so no travelling which was brilliant and a longer lie in every morning . Our days off school were spent in our local parks we had a few, Govanhill park, Brennan square and our lovely Queen's Park which all our summer holidays from school were spent.

Our nights were spent in many of our local cafe's mainly the bluebird which is still here to this day with the same lovely family owning it.

Govanhill in they days had a great sense of community everyone knew each other and the area felt safe for us. Victoria rd had every kind of shop that was needed from butchers, grocers to clothes and shoe shops we didn't even need to go into the town centre to get an outfit to go to our many local pubs and our famous plaza ballroom where we spent most of our Saturday nights after a drink in our local pubs mainly the Pandora or Maxwell arms, the Star bar and also McNees .

My job on leaving school was even on Victoria rd in a local lawyers office which was great, no bus fares to fork out from my wages. I married a local guy and had my three kids while still living in Govanhill an area my kids loved growing up in.

After my marriage broke down I sadly had to leave the area and moved out to Mansewood which then seemed like the other side of the world as I knew no one and all my family and friends were still in Govanhill but over the next few years I noticed when visiting Govanhill that it was going right downhill, the area was dirty, streets were overrun with rubbish the crime rate was getting very high and it was very overcrowded with fifty four nationalities in that one square mile and no integration to help people settle, our pensioners were getting mugged daily in broad daylight.

At that time my niece started up a campaign where they begged and pleaded the authorities for help to get the area back to a safe clean place to live and visit, but they done nothing so me and my life long pal Frannie decided to come on board and we marched with hundreds of our neighbours to local MSP and councillors offices to demand action, we roped in local papers and media to help us with our campaign, sad to see that since we started campaigning in 2012, now it's 2019 and we're still fighting for the same things and as long as my mum has to live in Govanhill we will continue to fight for her and her neighbours right to live and enjoy the area we're she brought up all her kids.

Simon Rose

Auld Govan toon
by Simon Rose

Auld Govan toon, o' shipyard fame, you've got a Facebook site
And it shows a lot o photos and stuff, that brings us great delight.
Your sons a daughter's have spread their wings to many far off places
But it's nice to know they can get on line, an see some familiar faces.

But, OMG! you wouldn't think things would have changed so much
Everyone now has a mobile phone, so that they can keep in touch.
But does that make things better, I fain would let you know
Back when we talked more face to face some fifty years ago.

Rejoice, Govanites rejoice, your life is now more fun
We have our parents to thank for that and all that they have done.
So thank your loved ones every day and fill their lives with cheer
And you'll never suffer regret or pain when the time comes they're
not here.
You'll always be my spiritual home and I'll never forget your name
You're in my heart, you're in my soul, you're the toon, o' shipyard
fame.
So I'll wish you well for the future with benefits galore
For your sons and daughter's happiness today and evermore.

Martha Evers

[This story was sent into me by Catherine Shields who is the niece of Martha. She found a lot of written notes by Martha and I have tried to put them together to give us an idea of Martha's life and preserve her memory and family's memory at the same time.]

Martha Evers is my name and 14 - Rose Street, [which later became Florence street] was our single end. This must have been the early 20s. The furniture my parents possessed was a table and one chair, that was it.

The table at one time must have had three knots running down the middle, now it has three holes. There was an empty space where the cutlery drawer should have been.

We called the table "The Holy Table". There was a long plain old wooden bunker, a coal bunker and an old black grate. A hole in the wall bed and a cupboard with three shelves. The walls were a red ochre colour at the top half and the bottom a very dark green paint, cracks everywhere. Bugs everywhere. This was home to us.

A very small single end it was too, no gas, only paraffin oil and candles. That was our light when it got dark. The floor was bare boards.

Six of us. Ma and Da, Annie, James, Martha and John all slept together on the hole in the wall, all squeezed together. It was certainly a case of you breath in and I'll breath oot.

Every time the chair (my Father's) was lifted to sweep underneath, one of the legs fell off. Father never thought to hammer in a nail. The leg just got pushed back in until the next time it was moved.

On the outside of the door to our wee single end in 14-Rose Street, was a wee iron disc to show how many people lived there. It said, two and a half adults. There were six of us, plus Jenny the hen. When going out, no-one locked their door, a cloth was jammed between the door, that was the house key. Never had a break in, had nothing to steal.

Some closes in Rose Street were numbered in half's.26 ½, 48 1/2, 52 1/2.

People hanging over their windows watching everything pass by. Policemen with their spiked helmets. Women standing at close mouth, breast hanging out feeding the wean. This was never looked on as being Indecent. To us the wean was just having its dinner.

Woman passed by wearing shawls and bare feet, coming from the wash house in Rutherglen Road, after doing a washing for someone better off... I'm just back fae the wash house they would say. Am gon doon tae Mathers Pub noo fur a hauf pint of beer. I remember the little cans for the beer in their hands, their hair wet hanging over their faces. You never saw a woman smoking in the street and they were never seen in pubs.

When St. Patrick's day came along, we children at school were given little harps, lovely little things. I remember them shaped like a harp, green ribbon entwined and a little green bow on top and little gold threads which was supposed to be the strings of the harp. This was the day we were asked are you a Billy or a Dan. If the boys were from Adelphie Terrace School, me and ma pals would shout "am a Dan, am a Dan" then run off for our lives. This was the only day we were a Billy or a Dan. The rest of the year we didn't bother. I sometimes went to mass, sometimes to confession, nothing to confess except that I had missed mass or I had been too sleepy to say my prayers before going to sleep.

When kneeling on the bare floors at the side of my fathers wee single iron bed, sometimes I got fed up praying. It would take so long, a Hail Mary for Maw and Da, a Hail Mary for my sister Annie, a Hail Mary for my brother James, a Hail Mary for my brother John, then I would remember someone else, a Hail Mary for him or her. I was on my knees so long I was fed up praying. My father used to think I had fallen asleep, hey Martha get into your bed.

189

When I went to Benediction, I felt really holy, the candles, the singing, the smell of incense. I felt I am in God's house. I went to Chapel in the morning for Spiritual comfort, then over to the Tent Hall for a feed. The priest could curse me or do what he likes, I thought, food was more important to me than his curse.

In the winter we got a bowl of soup, a thick piece of bread, then hymns, and prayers. In the summer we got a bowl of rice and thick bread. We always took a tin can with us to get it filled for our parents. Sunday morning breakfast for the poor, the hall was full of people. Two thick slices of bread, cheese, and a mug of tea.

New years treat for adults also. The Tent Hall was a wonderful place, wonderful people. Tea and slides every Saturday night. Sometimes I would put an old shawl round my head and shoulders to pretend I was an adult, I never got turned away. At Christmas word got around when the Tent Hall was handing out tickets for their Christmas treat. We went there for a feed and the toys, not to listen to the Gospel. We were hungry and we wanted food.

The chemist shop in Crown Street. Large different coloured goblets in the window. As the three golden balls were the sign of the pawnbroker, the large coloured goblets were the sign of the chemist.

On one wall, rows of little brown drawers, each drawer had a little sticker telling the contents of the drawer. Large jars different coloured powder also with stickers. Powder for the wean when teething "Turkey Rhubarb" was for the weans stomach, I think and If one got constipated, the chemist on Crown street is where they went.

I remember clearly mah Maw taking me there once. Mah wee lassie's constipated Mr. so and so. Chemist - Oh aye, I'll soon put her right and into the back shop he would go. Come back with a tumbler, into the tumbler he would then pour this brown stuff called "Senna tea". Jist drink this doon hen an you'll be awright. Standing at the counter I drank the stuff, very sweet I thought. If I remember correctly I had to make a bee line home at the double, mother trailing after me. Later on, are you awright now Martha hen? Aye Maw, 'am awright noo.

Mother got her new house in 101 Logan Street. All the neighbours in Rose Street were excited to find out where they would be moving to. Hannah was one of my mother's closest friends, she lived directly below my mother. How sad after living in the same close for all these years.

I hope I get beside you said Hannah. I was near to tears by this time having to say goodbye to all my pals.

I was about sixteen or seventeen by then, we had all grown up together. Was this really goodbye. The thought of moving to a new house with a bathroom made the move a bit easier.

Hannah got word she was moving to McNeil Street, my mother got word she was moving to Logan Street. On the day of the flitting all that was needed was a barrow to take was the Holy Table, one chair, a couple of black mattresses and that was our lot.
At sixteen/seventeen I was going to have my first bath with hot water, not a stick fire, but a coal fire. It was sheer luxury just lying there in awe that hot water, no hivin tae staun shivering at the auld sink anymair.

When my parents got their new house in Logan Street, one of the first things my mother bought was a brass nameplate for the door, it read. F. EVERS. Many a time the F caused a laugh.

During the war years, Martha her big sister Annie both from Logan Street along with other women and Italian prisoners of War worked in the Polmadie sheds. Martha's husband had died suddenly leaving her to bring up their two sons on a widows pension of ten shillings a week (50p). Even with her wages it was a struggle to bring up her two boys. Part of their job was to get down Into the pots where the men stood to repair underneath the trains. The women had to stand in piles of ashes, soot and water. Life was hard, money was short because footwear had to be replaced continuously.

191

Martha had to pawn her wedding ring, thinking she would be able to get it back, she didn't. One day she picked up the courage to speak to the head man. She told him about how much of her wages she had to spend on replacing footwear.

He was very understanding and the next day, everyone was given clogs to wear. When the engines and smoke boxes came into the sheds to be cleaned or repaired, there was barrow loads of soot and ashes which was dropped into the pits. The washer-outs came with their water hose to wash everything out.

All the water would swirl down into the pits among the soot and ashes and Martha's job along with the other women, was to climb down into the pits with their shovels and try to keep the pits clean, so the repair men could get on with their work. When the war ended, the women were no longer needed and had to say goodbye to their Italian friends.

They never saw them as enemies, even though they couldn't understand each other, they got by, by using their own form of sign language. There was much sadness as many of these friendships were of a very close nature.

Annie and Martha had two brothers away to war, James and John. The boys would send letters regularly to their maw, Mrs Evers and although Maw Evers loved all her children, she had a soft spot for John, the youngest.

Not only was he the youngest but John was taken in by the Evers family as a baby. His mother, a wee Irish lassie was only here three months when John was born in Barnhill poorhouse. She was befriended by a girl named Catherine who offered to help Mary find a home for John whilst she worked.

Mrs Evers, Rose Street, offered to take in John and let Mary work. There were 32 families in 14-Rose Street, all poor but Mrs Evers reached out to Mary who within a few years emigrated to Australia with the intention of sending for John who was now six years of age.

They never heard from her again and John, who was never fostered or adopted was brought up by the Evers as one of their own. Fed, clothed and showered with unconditional Love.

The letters from James continued but there was nothing at all from John. The dreaded news arrived, John was missing in action, presumed dead. For over ten months Maw Evers and Annie and Martha mourned their brother.

One day while Martha and Annie was at work in the Polmadie sheds, a troop train was passing through which was not unusual, but this day as the train slowed down the girls heard a voice shouting Annie, Martha, Annie, Martha.

The train continued slowly through the station. The girls looked at each other and started screaming. By this time the train was still going, the voice not as loud but Annie and Martha, although they hadn't seen their brother, they knew it was him. They dropped their buckets and mops and still screaming, ran home to 101 Logan Street to tell their Maw her wee blue eyed boy wasn't dead after all.

Maw Evers didn't believe them until John walked in the door after jumping from the train further down the line.

~~~~~

So ends the story of Martha Evers and thanks to Catherine Shields for sending me in the notes and slips of paper that her Auntie Martha had written down all those many years ago.

193

Billy Jock Litterick

My father was born and bred in Townhead, and my mother was a Possilpark girl. When they got married, they settled down in Springburn. Home was 4 Ayr Street, Springburn Glasgow. I was born there one balmy September day in 1952, but I don't remember much about it because I was very young at the time.

The Springburn of the 1950's and 60's was a bustling district of humanity. A cohesive structure of working class families in a bustling industrial district. The district itself was built around the manufacture and repair of steam locomotives. The first locomotive manufacturing and repair facility was built in 1842 at Cowlairs by the Edinburgh and Glasgow Railway. The second works was built in 1856 by the Caledonian Railway at St Rollox for the construction and repair of its rolling stock.

The other two works, Hyde Park, (established 1837), and Atlas, (1884), were both built to manufacture locomotives for export all over the world. The two firms merged in 1903 to become the North British Locomotive Company, (we knew it as NB Loco).

The NB Loco failed to make the transition from steam to diesel engines, and so closed its doors in 1962. The Cowlairs works had not built a locomotive since 1923 although it was used for servicing and repairs until 1968 when it closed its doors and transferred its business to St Rollox.

So Springburn, built on the back of the locomotive industry saw a steady decline from 4000 workers on the day-shift and 3000 on the night-shift in 1955, to 300 workers in 1992.

My earliest recollection is of sitting on the steps at the entrance to our close singing, "Ah'm four tomorrow hahaha, ah'm four tomorrow hahaha..." I don't know how long I sat there, but can you imagine a mother allowing her three year old child out of her sight for any length of time nowadays? She'd be beside herself. That was the innocence of the age – a more genteel, simple age.

Springburn was a wonderful place to grow up in the 1950's and 60's, and our patch was the best, although I bet every Springburn kid will say the same thing about their own patch!

Our tenement, a four storey red sandstone block was situated at the end of Mollinsburn Street, opposite Hydepark School and adjacent to Paddy's Park, where we spent long balmy never ending summers playing football and flying kites and throwing our arrows made from a penny cane with a dart feather for a flight, and even longer freezing winters, sledging all the way down the park slope to the Adamswell Street back yards.

By the 1960's, the beautiful old Victorian buildings that housed the locomotive manufacturing facilities were empty and derelict, and had become the occasional playgrounds of the neighbourhood children. From the enormous workshops where we would climb up the steel columns and walk along the overhead crane gantries, to the Railwaymens' Club in Atlas Street, everywhere was our playground.

I remember one day, we found treasure. It was a mound of molten blue glass of some sort. Around it was small pebbles of the stuff. "Diamonds," whispered Garry Caldwell, all of us nodding assent. "Maybe they were dropped by robbers and they're gonny come back for them," says I. So we done the right thing – we gathered it all up and took it round to the police station in Gourlay Street. As we walked into the charge office, the big desk sergeant loomed over us. We dutifully, (and fearfully), handed over the, "diamonds," but sad to say, they were but glass. How exciting is a young lad's outlook on life.

My dad sadly passed away in 1962 leaving my mum to bring us up. David was 17; Ian was 14 and I was 9. She got a job cleaning across the road at Hydepark School clinic which she done from 1962 until her own death in 1970.

We just don't comprehend how hard life was in those days. I still remember the first week she started there, the whole of the top of her right arm was black and blue from the exertion. She started work at 5:30am until 9am., and then from 4pm to 6 pm, and Saturday mornings from 8am to 11am. Her pay was just over £7 a week, and it was blood and sweat money.

On Saturday morning, it was my job to do the messages. First stop was auld Archie's green grocers shop in Flemington street for the new potatoes.

Archie was a character. He was as blind as a bat. His glasses were as thick as bottle bottoms, and he used to use a magnifying glass as well to see the weights and measures he used on his scales.

The shopping list was always the same; 1/2lb of Ayrshire bacon, square slice; black pudding to name a few, and always last at the top of Springburn Road was a visit to the City Bakeries – strawberry tart was my mum's favourite whilst mine was the flee's graveyard.

Every Sunday morning at around 10am., the Salvation Army band would attack us with their trumpets, cymbals and the big oompah. They had a spot right under our first floor flat bedroom window where Ayr Street meets Mollinsburn Street, and they always played their heart out – much to our dismay sometimes. Fortunately we were always awake, because our Sunday morning reveille was the, "Billy Cotton Band Show," on the radiogram. The opening line was always, "Wakey wakey..." in a strong Cockney accent.

After breakfast, we three boys were dressed up in our Sunday best and it was off to Sunday School. The route was always the same, down Ayr Street; left into Adamswell Street; down the stairs to Valleyfield Street; right into Flemington Street; left into low Ayr Street and walk along to the end past the Hyde Park Works on the right and the Springburn Library on the left, which I think was donated by Andrew Carnegie, along with the Springburn Halls. Carrying on, we would go up the stairs to Springburn Road and then a couple of hundred yards to the Baptist church in Blenheim Street. On the way home, my

Sunday treat was to stand at the bridge over the railway line when the 2 o'clock train was pulling into the station below, and take in the rich smell of the steam from the engine.

As we got a bit older and a bit more independent, we used to go for long cycle rides out to the Campsie Hills – a journey of about 15 miles. I can't remember how long the trip took, but those were wonderful days out.

We would take packed lunches with us and spend the day there. Parking our bicycles at the bottom of the Campsies, (Milton of Campsie), we would explore the hills, looking for a downed Messerschmidt that was rumoured to be there. We never found it though. The amazing thing was, when we got back to the bicycles to return home, they were always there. No one had tried to steal them. No one had fiddled with them at all. The 1960's surely was a golden era that's not coming back.

Going to primary school was a dawdle! I would wait until 5 minutes before the bell rang and then saunter slowly across the street to the playground, satchel on my back and skull cap on head, except if it was winter, then it would be a balaclava. Being at school was sometimes something different. I still remember Mrs Hare, one of our primary school teachers. She was the bane of many a pupil's life. If she caught you talking in class or being otherwise not on your best behaviour, various missiles would suddenly start to get bigger as they found their way through the air towards you. Anything at hand would do for Mrs Hare, from chalk to blackboard dusters. I'm sure she would be carted away kicking and screaming in the white van nowadays.

After primary school, I went up the Albert senior secondary school. Now that was different. no more lying in bed until 8:15 and leisurely breakfasts.

The Albert was a bus ride to the top of Springburn Road, then a walk up Northcroft Road and Campsie Street to the school. I have many good memories from that school. Like the time we were sitting in the applied mechanics class and the teacher, Davy Eason was writing on the blackboard. One of the boys in the class made a paper aeroplane out of some drawing paper and set it to flight. Unfortunately, it hit Davy Eason on the back of the head. The expletives are redacted, but the remainder of his sentence was, "It's like farting against thunder trying to teach you lot."

The Boys' Brigade played a big part in my life growing up. I was in the 202nd at Springburn Baptist church. Friday night was the main BB night with Tuesday night being gym night. I remember waiting at the bus stop with Garry Caldwell one Friday night in 1966, on our way to the BB and we were talking about the Aberfan disaster. After the BB, we would go to Santi's fish and chip shop at the corner of Hill Street and Springburn Road, and sit in and have a packet of chips and a coffee.

The highlight of the week however, was the Saturday morning football game in the BB league. We had a great football team, and we won the Glasgow league four times in a row.

Harry Wilson had a body swerve that left everyone standing, and John Donaldson was right back as hard as Bobby Shearer or Eric Caldow [the Glasgow Rangers full backs of that era]. We then went on to win the Glasgow church league once before I hung up my boots for the pub on Friday nights.

At the bottom of Springburn Road was Vulcan Street, and on the corner of Vulcan Street and Springburn Road was the Vulcan pub. One starry Friday night around 1969 as the bus was going past the Vulcan, there was a rumpus going on and two black Maria vans and two ambulances. I heard the story later:

Some chaps had been sitting at a table in the public bar playing dominoes, when in walked the local thug big Malky – not his real name.

Big Malky was carrying a concealed weapon on his person - an axe. Looking casually around the public house, his eyes lighted upon the one for whom he was looking, (wee Jimmy - the chap who had put his

198

sister Maggie up the duff). Wee Jimmy was one of the chaps playing a friendly game of dominoes with some other boundha's.

Big Malky walked casually up to said table and, withdrawing his axe whilst at the same time shouting words which could not possibly be shared here, proceeded to plant the offending weapon in the heid of wee Jimmy who, upon hearing big Malky's guttural war cry, swung his head round to see what the commotion was about. As it turned out, this was just as well, because said weapon was then planted in wee Jimmy's shoulder instead of his head.

In the rumpus which followed, the patrons of the bar set about big Malky in a manner fitting of a Glasgow Friday night at the pub.

It was not long after, that my number 45 bus, taking me home from the Boys' Brigade, drove slowly past the scene. As I said, there were two ambulances there - one for wee Jimmy with the hatchet embedded adjacent to his clavicle, and the other for big Malky, who, as it turned out had received several moothfaes of wee heidies, as well as several steel toe capped shoes to some unmentionable parts.

In 1967, we moved from our tenement to a new flat in Pinkston Drive, Sighthill. The block was brand new so everything smelt of newness; the concrete, the brickwork; the plaster and the paint. There was a row of tenements left in Springburn Road opposite St Rollox, after the main demolition, and the dairy there was where I would run down to every morning and buy half a dozen well fired rolls for our breakfast before going to school.

It was the new way of life and, "High Living,' was on TV to prove it. When mum died in 1970, I was on my own, so my elder brother Ian and his new wife Betty came to stay with me. They had bought their own flat in lower Ayr Street a couple of years before, but gave it up for me.

I left school in 1970 after Highers and joined British Steel Corporation as a trainee metallurgist. Every night at around quarter to nine, Ian and I would take a walk from the Sighthill flat along Springburn Road to the Vulcan, where we would have two pints and walk home again at 10 o'clock closing time. One spring night when we were walking to the pub, there was a bunch of yobo's on the other side of the road coming the other way. As they started crossing the road towards us, one of them shouted, "Peg ya bas!" My brother looked at them and shouted back, "Police ya bas!" That stopped them dead in their tracks, and they turned round and walked away. We were both wearing dark blue overcoats so we must've looked the part.

In November 1971, we left Springburn and Glasgow and Scotland behind and emigrated to South Africa. I'm still here in Durban – through the thick and thin of it. Life has been good here if you disregard the politics. I've been in the consulting field for 30 years now, after my time in the Fire Brigade where I left as a divisional officer. I've worked on projects throughout Africa from Kenya and Tanzania to Zimbabwe and Zanzibar, and in other parts of the world such as Azerbaijan.

I lost my wife in 2002 and my brother Ian in 1998. My eldest brother David is still in Scotland, and I've been married to Arlene now for 16 wonderful years.

If I had it all to do over again and had a choice of places to grow up, I would pick Springburn every single time.

Thomas "Tam" Rodgers

Life in Royston growing up.

My name is Thomas Rodgers born in 1939 I grew up with my two sisters and three brothers in a three bedroom flat in Roystonhill rd, life was great I loved our community and went to St Rochs primary school where I made life long pals.

I then moved on to St Rochs secondary in the area too, then left at fifteen to start my first job as a milk boy in Royston and loved earning my first wage even though our tips were paid in ginger bottles but I still felt rich.

I met my wife Helen at eighteen but left Royston to join the R.A.F. and travelled the world for four years mostly in Germany. When I left the R.A.F I married Helen and had our two children Thomas and Jacqueline who were raised in Royston My second job was in the gasworks to provide for my family.

After my marriage broke down I left Glasgow to seek a life in London but I couldn't settle there so I moved to Manchester, alone and with nothing, so I ended up sleeping on the streets where I met people who became the only family I knew and helped me through so many rough times. I managed with my new friends to find casual work.

My sister traced me through the Salvation Army and came down to Manchester and brought me back to Glasgow but I couldn't settle again and shortly after returned to Manchester where me and a friend thought we'd hit the jackpot when a smartly dressed man spoke to us at the Salvation Army and offered us a job looking after horses on the Isle of Man.

The next day we were on a ferry thinking we were heading to Isle of Man but it turned out we were getting took to Belfast and turned out the guy was a gypsy and took us to his camp-site where we had to work for them and sleep in a lorry, eventually after numerous attempts we managed to escape them and fled back to Manchester where I lived on the streets again, working casual and getting looked after by the sisters at the convent, life was hard but it's all I knew then.

As I got older my health deteriorated and my sister and ex wife talked me into coming back to Glasgow to be with my family which I'm happy to say I did, and I'm now back in Royston in the bosom of my kids and grand-kids. I have a lovely wee flat in James Nesbitt st in Royston just a few closes down from my ex Helen and I see my kids and grand-kids regularly and spend my free time walking all over the streets of Glasgow just glad to be home again where I belong.

Catherine Shields

CLABBER PIES

I remember growing up in Possilpark with great fondness. In the summer a man would come round with a pony and trap and for a penny would take us round the block and then there was the rag man who gave you a lovely big balloon in exchange for yer mammys fur coat... My early years it seems, was spent mostly outdoors, oot the back. My Mother would give me a big spoon from the cutlery drawer (which was put back after I finished digging with it, cleaned of course) and an empty tin can which was kept in the bathroom...The tin can was very versatile ..It was used to empty the toilet pan then my mum would give the pan a good scrub wae VIM...It was also used in the bath or the sink to rinse our hair after shampooing, (no showers in those days and before the contraption which had three major parts, two of them you shuved oan the taps and the other bit was the shower head.) It was better than the tin can, except when the bloody thing blew aff because of the water pressure.....After all my digging, I would climb the rone pipe outside our kitchen window, even though I was only about two or three years of age and shout for my mum to fill the can with water, this allowed me to make my Clabber Pies. When I got a wee bit older, instead of clabber pie making, I would sit for hours on the grass and make daisy chains. Necklaces, bangles, hair bands or belts or one in my hair, kept in place with a Kirby.

Then I progressed to wee shops. Come and buy, Come and buy, my shop's open.. again this included dirt.. This time the tin cans were rescued from the midden then filled up with dirt and displayed on my mums living room window sill. I also kept dirt aside in case someone wanted a lb of mince or stew which was wrapped in old newspaper. I also sold fish and chips, this was large dock leaves for the fish and Timothy grass for the chips.(Only found out these names recently) We used pieces of broken china which had a gold rim but better than that and had more value, was the coloured glass, usually black or green. It was smooth on one side and ribbed on the other. I gave up my wee shop when my till broke. It was a silvery green colour, with a hammered finish and red button keys.

I remember White clover flowers which grew in the back, we called them mulkies. The older kids told us if ye sooked them you could get milk from them...Naw yea didney...Then there was Buttercups which you held under a friend's chin to see if they liked butter. A didnae go near the Dandelions, they made yea pee the bed. I remember the outdoor concerts, you brought a stool or cushion with you and paid a penny to get in...Paid a Penny tae get in....It was an outdoor concert.. When I was three years old, the older kids decided to walk to the swing park in Oakbank lane, which was one and a half miles away. The only thing I remember was being brought home by the police, I was able to tell them my name and address. They stopped off at the Tallies and bought me a poakie hat....My mum didn't even know I was away, she thought i was still digging in the back...Some of the street games we played included, once again, dirt. When playing chalk beds, if you didn't have a piece of marble to slide along the pavement you could use an empty shoe polish tin, filled with dirt, which made it heavy and easier to use. It was only the girls who played beds or skipping ropes or ball games, which was played on the City Glass Work wall, which was in Denmark Street. Denmark Street was great for roller-skating. If your pal didn't have roller skates you loaned them one of yours. It was ok with one but a whole lot better with two. Us kids lived dangerously back then. We would jump from the wee midden shelter and leap up to the big air raid shelter. For some reason we called them dykes. Wee dykes and Big dykes. We would even venture up to the High backs were the Dykes were more scary. From the midden you leapt on to a high wall which had a curved top. Your feet were at a funny angle but then you had to stand still then leap again on to another big dyke. If you fell, well that was you in hospital. The only way to complete the jumps was by wearing sandshoes or bumpers, they gave you a good grip. Sometimes we would walk the railings which separated the backs, you had to be very careful, wan slip. Yer right fit gone wan wie, yer left the other .O YA.. Some of the games we played were. Wan man hunt. Hide and seek. Kick the can. Please sir may I cross the water...Aunties and Uncles.. We played Stankie wae jorries, there was always the wan boy who managed tae win everybody's bools, and of course Swapping Scraps, Angels with big wings, Cherubs all sizes, Santa Clause's, Crinoline lady's, but this was just something the girls did. We also played Chinese ropes. A great game to play was Burrlie...yea burrelled roon and roon until yea got dizzy, then stoated aboot the back, bumping into anything and oanything. You could play this game yourself but it was better if there were a few of ye's, wit a laugh bumping aff each other. The game I hated most was Truth, Dare, Double Dare, Promise, Kiss or Torture.......

The boys were always playing football in the street, never the lassies, well there was one, Madge, she was better than some of the boys, she wore a leather helmet and years later, went round the street with a horse and cart selling brickets...

Going back to when I was wee, I remember my dad would take a piece of rope, double it and tie it through the railings. He then got my mums coat, put it over the ropes and fastened it to make a hammock. I could spend ages in there, looking up at the clouds. I still love looking at the clouds to this day.

Our milk was delivered by Sammy Strachan and his horse and cart and when my dad was in a gardening mood we were given a bucket and shovel and made to run after the hoarse n gaither up the manure. My dad had the best display of tulips in the whole of Possil...

Saracen Street was the main shopping area. There was the Cowlairs Co-op for your general messages, tea, bread, eggs, butter. My mum would buy a plain loaf and a French pan, there was also the Co-op butchers, chemist and a very large Co-op which sold clothing, furniture, haberdashery.

There was Britons, Reid's and Galloway's butchers. Agnue the fish mongers, Mc Cann's fruit shop. There were two other chemists. We also had Hubbard's, Craigs and the Electric bakery. Hubbard's sold the best triffles and Craigs sold the best Pear Squares.

We had two DIY stores, Forresters and Danny Kays. Quigley's and McManus's pawn salerooms. McManus's also sold ladies, gents and children's wear. There was four ice cream shops and three or four chippies. We had Curleys, Masseys, Templetons and Galbraiths, for such a short street it had an amazing amount of shops. There were umpteen newsagents, dairy's, hairdressers, dentists and Montgomery and Balloch who were husband and wife doctors who's surgery was in Bardowie Street.

A red police box stood at the corner of Bardowie Street and Saracen Cross.

Within the block of closes where I lived were two gable ends. In one of them, every now and again a large plank of wood would appear over the top of the railings.

What fun we had on that see-saw, except when you got a skelf or skelves oan yer thigh. Never found out where the plank of wood came from or where it went when it wasn't there.

My primary school was St. Theresa's and in my class was a boy called Willie Carr who went on to play football for Coventry City and also played six full international matches for Scotland.

The actor Peter Capaldi also went to my school and Lena Martell came from Possilpark. My first job was a junior Clerkess in a Sawdoctors. I had to walk from my close to my workplace which took just over two minuets. There were Hand saws, back saws, hack saws, Tennon saws, Circular saws, Ripp saws, they were sharpened or re toothed. I made up the wages and kept the books. Enjoyed my time there, plenty of banter.

Kathy Huet

I was born in Robroyston Hospital, Glasgow on the 10th of August 1954 to Anna and Matthew Mailey.

Life started quite the opposite to most folks at that time as I entered into the great life of the sprawling housing scheme of Garthamlock, at the tender age of 3 months old, a concession given to my parents as my Mum had previous health issues.

Great memories of green fields, new school buildings and modern housing.

Due to family problems my Mum had to move us to another home in Maryhill, traumatic stuff leaving our friends and my brother Martin was so into his football at school too, what a wrench. Injury to insult- Martin was quite talented which we learnt later as he was subsequently flown down to sign an "S" form with Aston Villa. However Mums said no you're too young at 15 years old, get your O levels boy.

It was a Culture shock - indeed moving to Maryhill but like most kids we adapted to our new life Even though we had no green fields close by, we had old school buildings like Garnethill convent where I started my secondary education and worst of all the dreaded outside toilet but on the plus side, new pals, youth club facilities a picture hall close by and of course the thrill of Firhill park just up the road.

Life was good once again. I married at age 21 and emigrated to South Africa early 1976, had triplet sons Craig, Raymond and Ross in 1978 in Johannesburg and treated like celebrities by these wonderful South Africans.

Unfortunately I have only been back to Glasgow once since 1979. One day in particular holds such a happy memory for me, as we were pushing our boys in their buggies up Garscube rd and out of nowhere a number 60 bus halts and the passengers come streaming off to say hello to us, such joy and laughter and a great welcome home.

This is to me typical of the friendly humorous people of Glasgow.

Back to South Africa, where my dear Mum and brother eventually joined us and a very happy life here too. I remarried an Irishman, a remarkable man, his name is Mark who has been a great Dad to our boys and of course the cherry on top was the birth of our youngest son Ryan in 1989.

Ryan and Caitlin have just become proud parents to our beautiful grandson Craig Charles Huet, born on the 4th of March 2019. My ambit is to walk down Garscube rd again with wee Craig as he is also a bus stopper, and introduce him to some of the best folks in the world.

PS
I am still asked regularly if I am enjoying my holiday in South Africa as I still haven't lost my Glasgow accent, I'm so very proud of that. AYE it's been a long holiday lol.

Chapter 14

Castlemilk

Castlemilk

Extracts from the book - "The Big Flit"

Life before Castlemilk, memories of the old tenements.

Most people who came to live in Castlemilk were leaving behind a "room and kitchen" or even a "single end"in the old tenements, with no bathroom and used a shared toilet on the stair landing. The kitchen was where you lived, cooked, ate and slept.

The fire was a coal fire in the middle of a big black leaded Stanley range, on either side of this was a cooking area and the bed was in a recess in the kitchen. Years ago people used to do their washing in the boiler room in the back-court but later lots of them would use the public washhouse or "The Steamie" as it was more commonly called, it was all hard work for our Mothers, Granny's and great Granny's.

Usually you had an old zinc bath that you washed in once a week and all the family used the same [dirty] water, that was how we lived back in the days of the tenements. Then all of a sudden about ten years after the end of WWII there were these new housing schemes getting built and they had an inside toilet and bathroom and a balcony!!

So the story I am about to tell is just about one of these new housing schemes which was called Castlemilk. It is an edited very short summing up of the book "The Big Flit". I have given full acknowledgement and thanks to all who were involved in this book at the end of the story as I certainly don't want to violate any copyright material.

"I remember the day the card came through the door telling me I had a house in Castlemilk, that was in 1957, I was so excited, I was getting a "New house" that I ran out to telephone my Mother, I just couldn't wait. Then my husband came home from work and he was over the moon too. We both went to the hight street housing office the next morning but only my husband signed the form. He had to take a day off from work without pay but we didn't mind about that!!

We also had to sign a form stating whether we wanted gas or electricity services. Water was connected and we were to get hot water from our coal fire. The electricity board could put in an immerser but you had to pay for that yourself. We got missives for our house which gave us the regulations for payments of rent and rates and things like cleaning the streets. We paid our rent every quarter, £8 it was, we had only paid £1-7/- in our old house in Cowcaddens. We got a ground floor house, it was a corner house in Ardmaleish rd and it had a big garden, we were over the moon. I have never once regretted moving to our Castlemilk home". **Rose McLean**

"I moved to Castlemilk from Polmadie in April 1956, it was midday and all our belongings, furniture etc were piled in the van, I was really excited and the weans had a rerr terr. The men brought our furniture in to our new home, I had a utility bedroom suite, it was really solid with a great big wardrobe. It took a bit of maneuvering to get it in so they dumped it in the living room. They took the beds and other things upstairs. When the men left my husband and brother tried to move the wardrobe, they tried all ways-upside-down, sideways but it wouldn't move. Luckily my husband was a Joiner, he took the whole thing to bits, marked each bit, left hand, right hand and the back etc and carried it bit by bit up the stairs. He put it together again in the bedroom, it's still there to this day. I don't know what will happen if we had to move again, I think I would leave it". **Isa Roberts**

"Nobody moved on a Saturday as it was supposed to be bad luck, I often wonder about those folks who moved in, stayed for a wee while and then just disappeared, leaving the house empty and a brand new house too!! There were no amenities, no shops, practically no schools and extra bus fares. When people came to Castlemilk there was a tremendous change to their lives, some people couldn't take the shock, others couldn't afford it, we were like early settlers.

We needed an extra wage for bus-fares to go to visit our families who were all over in another part of town. Children had problems to as they had to be bussed all over to their old schools. Some kept up social activities in their old districts like the boys brigade for instance and that mean more bus-fares. A lot of women went out to work when their children got older". **Ina Lynch**

Allocation of new houses
You didn't get to pick your new house, your name was put in, and lots were drawn to allocate you to a specific house. However people with medical reasons could be allocated a ground floor house.

Losing family connections
It was sad to be moving away from the place where you were born and brought up and where your family lived either up the next close or nearby.

Stages of Castlemilk
The early years of the building of Castlemilk was around Arnprior, Glenacre drive,, stretching to the bottom of Castlemilk drive. This happened between 1954-55.

Then by 1956 there was the beginnings of Ardencraig drive, Bogany terrace, the top part of Castlemilk drive and down Tormusk rd.

The last bits were around Birgidale, Downcraig, Dunagail, Drakemire and Raithburn. The earliest houses to be occupied were Arnprior quad, part of Glenacre, part of Dougrie drive, part of Machrie between January and December 1955.

After that around Arnprior, Croftfoot, Cavine, the bottom of Castlemilk drive and a bit in Ardencraig quad and rd.

Design of Housing
There was a bit of friction between the Scottish office and Glasgow corporation about the design of the houses, possibly because they were under the impression that Glasgow people wanted tenement style

houses. There was never any consultation with the tenants over the planning of any aspect in Castlemilk.

The High flats
The multi-storeys were built in the 1960's and the early 70's at the same time they were going up all over Britain.

Social needs
There was an assumption that families rather than other groups were to be catered for in this type of housing provision.
The main priority was for families from the inner city areas because their houses were too small or because they were unfit for habitation eg: the clearance of the Gorbals and Govan.

Digging gardens
Every tenant in our bit had their own wee piece of garden. Everybody helped each other. **Isa Robertson**

Kitchen, Bathrooms and Balconies
My second home in Castlemilk was in Birgidale ave in 1966 and just like my first house it was great to have a kitchen. In our other house in Oatlands, you lived, ate and slept in the same room. There was a cooker, a big washing tub, a sink, a drying cupboard, a larder and a broom cupboard. There was a gas boiler to boil clothes and there was a pulley for hanging clothes to dry.

Later on we put in an electric immerser for hot water. We thought we were Toff's when we set the table in the living room. **Peggy McCauley**

We really couldn't get over having a balcony, we had a lovely view and we had the sun all day from early morning to late at night and plenty of fresh air too. **Ina Lynch**

It was a luxury to have a bathroom with a bath in it. I could have a bath any time I liked, but I told people since I've come to Castlemilk, I have a bath once a year, whether I need it or not!! **John Jamieson**

Transport

At first in the beginning most buses only came to Croftfoot roundabout, when you had a bus strike we had to walk it, **said a resident**

Shopping

We used to go to Croftfoot for shops or bought from the mobile vans, the vans charged extra and people had to pay through the nose. They also gave credit but you had to pay back an enormous amount. Shopping wasn't easy, there were so few shops mostly mobile vans or Croftfoot shops. Lots of people went back to their old areas to shop, it was difficult to change old ways.

Machrie rd shops.

Doctors etc

Some people stayed with their old doctors where they used to live, Doctors had no appointment system then. You could leave home in the morning with a sick child and not get back to late afternoon sometimes. Nearest hospital was the Victoria.

Entertainment

If you wanted to go to the cinema or the dance hall, you had to go out of Castlemilk. you maybe went to Shawlands or maybe Victoria rd in Govanhill or further afield into the Toon, but if you did you had to watch you didn't miss the last bus back to the housing scheme.

Castlemilk Tenants Association

Iris McDonald - said "I was one of the first tenants in Castlemilk, shortly after we moved in we canvassed around the doors and more or less everyone joined the T.A. One of the main aims back then was as the houses were still getting built we had no pavements to walk on, it was literally a huge building site. So we pressed for getting pavements put in and also put pressure on getting shops built in the area. She said that some of the other founding members of the T.A. were Mrs Hamilton, Frank Slater and David McWhinnie and they were all dear friends. Only thing she said was it was a great pity that when someone asked for a run-down on what the T.A. did, we never kept a written record and could only rely on our memory".

Authors note: This was just a very brief summarised account of what it must have been like for people who had lived in a tenement all their life and were told that they were to be given a house, with an inside toilet, a bath, a balcony, and possibly a garden or/and a wee plot to grow veg on, this was something they had never imagined possible, of course it did happen and this was so new and exciting back then.

Of course there are many various housing schemes spread all over the greater Glasgow area, I just opted to go for Castlemilk as the name of the book "Caslemilk" - "**The Big flit**" appealed to me. Yes as someone said they were the "Early settlers.

~~~~~~

It is, with sincere regret that the group records the death of John Jamieson, one of its founding members. The group are grateful to his wife Millie who has consented to have John's memories recorded in this publication.

Full acknowledgement and thanks to everyone mentioned below

The peoples history group would like to acknowledge the help, co-operation and support of the following people and organisations for their visits to the class with memories, photographs, information and stories.

The late Iris McDonald - Castlemilk Tenants Association.

Mrs Mamie Murphy and Rev John Miller-Castlemilk East Parish Church

Mrs Mima Reid and the Clergy- St Margaret Mary's R.C. Church.

Mr John McKechnie and the Rev Robert Wotherspoon-Castlemilk West Parish Church.

The Clergy of St Martin's R.C. Church.

The late Mrs McGraw for the story of "Frankie with the Hankie".

Jeanie Telfer- for her story.

Alex Erskine - for photos - Rab Patterson for drawings.

Nan Kerr for the story of her work in Castlemilk childrens home.

Ken McLeod - then senior development officer, city housing, Castlemilk

Elspeth King - the Peoples Palace.

The staff and children of St Margaret Mary's secondary school.

For their work and support
in the production of this book

Pat Chisolm and Mary McLaughlan - who faithfully and patiently transcribed our tape recordings and typed them.

COJAC and ADTEC - for use of equipment.

Margaret Stewart of the victim support scheme, for help with the computer.

Catherine Tait, Anne Fehilly and Irene Graham of safe Castlemilk for additional help.

Ian Miller and Frank McAvoy - city housing, Castlemilk, for additional information.

Paul Cameron - community education service for design and lay-out.

City housing, Castlemilk for funding for the book and Janice Curry for her help and advice.

Special thanks to:-
Margaret Urquart, the staff and committees of the Pensioners Action Centre for their unstinting encouragement and support.

Finally we must thank Alison Miller and the W.E.A. in Castlemilk, without who's wholehearted support for the project and help in editing of the material, this publication would not have been possible.

~~~~~~

The Author would also like to thank the Castlemilk local History group for all their help in assisting me with the "extracts" from the book "The Big Flit". I really do appreciate it.

Chapter 15

Extra - Bits

Irene [Donna] Robertson

Gaun tae the Pictures

Loved gaun tae the pictures long before tellys... sometimes three times a week or mer... the Wee Geggie in Brigton wiz the cheap wan for aw the weans.. they let ye in tae see Xs how they managed that a dont know but they did... it wiz always packed tae the rafters..on the wan level , well it did hiv whit they referrred tae as a balcony but mer a slant in the flerr wae better seats and a wee bit dearer.. a preferred them as ye wurnae squeezed up the widden benches tae get mer weans in like the stalls.. a mind wan day someone shoved the benches the gether and ma bum got jammed in between.. ye kin imagine the squeals during King Kong....Another day they let in too many and hid us actually sitting in the aisles then for some reason we got chipped oot.. by the scruff of the neck..never saw the cowie that wiz showing that day, think it wiz Audie Murphy anaw and a fancied him at the time..........at the winchin bits it wiz pandemonium wae the racket as naebody wiz interested.. they aw wanted the cavalry coming and saving the day wae their bugle ... and the Indians gettin done in... Same wae Captain Blood... the boys were aw up dummy fencin oan the benches ..and the chucker oots taking a wulkie and roaring and swearin at them tae sit doon .. A mind the Geggie getting "renovated" as they cawed it... they got a new front bigger front door put oan and hauf a lion in a gless case in the "foyer"..........whit fur ave never fun oot. but gave us something tae look it while we bote oor sweeties from the new wee shop ....funny thing is they never got roon to dain anything wae the horrible smelly toilet... so a made sure a went before the pictures...

Talking of dirty toilets the Kings anaw on James st wiz always overflowing.. ye hid tae paddle thru it aw and always hid a smell.......the usherettes wid come roon during the film and scoot us aw wae that disinfectant ye goat in a daurk green boatle at school .. ye d be sitting watching William Holden guffin of some concoction they forced on us..scootin it aw ower oor hair....Most of the picture halls were the heaving aroon the area apart fae the Olympia...noo this wiz

219

grandeur..whit a lovely hall and a clean toilet wae white seats... Id never seen white seats before and felt like a princess using them.. always immaculate and clean with deep purple and red carpets in the foyer and nice smells.. Everything aboot the Olympia I loved and had my last visit to it around the late 60s, think it was Women in Love they were showing that night... but the Minors on a Saturday morning wiz the highight of the week for weans.... big queues aw shouting and excited waiting to get in.. am sure the usherettes needed tranquilized efter it .. but great times wae Flash Gordon.. Zorro.. Roy Rogers. Famous Five. Abbot and Costello....oh a wish a wiz a wean again....

St Enoch's Sq

The Square sits on land that once was the western part of Glasgow green, alongside the river Clyde, and reportedly had a chapel and burial site of St Thenew (St Enoch) mother of St Kentigern.

The site changed hands to the Luke family of goldsmiths, managers of the soaperie in Candleriggs and owners of the glass-works next to the Clyde, who in turn sold it to the Merchants House of Glasgow, and from there to Glasgow City Council who laid the foundation stone of St Enoch Church in 1780. It is one of six squares in the city centre.

The square, always of a quiet and retiring nature then, was joined by grand Regency style buildings between around 1780-1820, the focal point south of the centre being St Enoch's Church, originally designed by James Jaffra in 1780.

The church was later substituted for another, this time designed by David Hamilton in 1827. The centre was planted with grass and shrubbery with an iron railing round it, and grazed with sheep. The grass plot remained till about 1860, when it was removed to make way for the farmers, who in that year, were prohibited from meeting in Stockwell Street on the Wednesday market-days. With increasing traffic and a congregation now living further away the church was demolished in 1926, in order to allow space for a bus terminus and car parking.

In the 1860s many streets, of houses, shops, warehouses, restaurants, hotels and inns, and theatres including the Theatre Royal in Dunlop Street and David Brown's Royal Music Hall, on the east side they were demolished to make way for the railway lines of the Glasgow & South Western railway Company crossing the Clyde. One of the major buildings on the square, which had to move, was the Faculty and Surgeons Hall of the Royal College of Physicians which moved to new premises 242 St Vincent Street where the College remains today. St. Enoch Station opened in 1876, with its St. Enoch Hotel opening in 1879. The hotel was then the largest hotel in Glasgow, with over 200 bedrooms. The station and hotel were both one of the first buildings to be lit by electricity in the city.

The hotel eventually closed in 1974, and was used as a car park until work began on the indoor St. Enoch centre in 1985, designed by Arup Associates and built by Sir Robert McAlpine & sons. A £150 million refurbishment programme began in 2005.

This work concluded in May 2010. Along with this work, St Enoch Square received an upgrade, transforming the area into a plaza like environment, housing large screens for broadcasting, and generally creating a more pleasant urban area for pedestrians.

Refurbishment of the St Enoch Underground, created in 1896, began in 2014, and was completed in 2015, in an attempt to create a more modern and efficient environment. The £5.3 million contract involved replacing the entrances to the subway with new entrance canopies made of glass and steel, replacement of the floor, wall and ceiling materials, and general upgrading of facilities and equipment.

"Ur - ye - Dancin?"

How many of us Glasgow men uttered those immortal words to the fairer sex when in one of the many dance halls that used to be all over the Toon and greater Glasgow area. I attended a few of these dance halls in my younger days.the Plaza at Eglinton toll, the Locarno and Majestc in the Toon but I have to say my favourite was the Barrowland on the Gallowgate.

On a Friday night I would get paid my wages and couldn't wait to get home to my parents house, have a hot bath and don my three piece suit, not forgetting to put a few dollops of Brylcream on my hair and off up the Gallowgate.

My first stop was to pay a visit to the "Saracen head" pub run back then by big Angus Ross [a Highlander and great guy]. I would order a pint of rough scrumpy cider [with bits of wood floating in it] and a glass of White Tornado wine and after being in there for about an hour or more it was cross over the road and queue up to get into the Barrowland dance hall and see if I could get a dance and maybe "chat up a bird". Was great doing the twist or a slow dance and Bingo at the end of the night if you got a lumber. You just hoped the lassie didn't live too far away [because you always escorted her home].

Oh and if the back close winchin was good you would ask her for a date the following night and you always tried to impress her with spending your hard earned money as if it was going out of fashion. Some of these "romances" only lasted one night while others could last a long time with you and the young lady becoming boyfriend/girlfriend. It was great having a girlfriend but after a while I wanted to be with my mates again, having a drink and "playing the field" again, so once more it was back to the "Sarry Heid" a pint of Scrumpy cider, glass of white Tornado, over to the Barrowland and "Ur ye Dancin". Oh to be young again eh!!

Woolworths

Woolworths Group was a listed British company that owned the High street retail chain Woolworths. It also owned other companies such as the entertainment distributor Entertainment UK, and book and resource distributor Bertram books.

The Woolworths store chain was the main enterprise of the group. Originally a division of the American F. W. Woolworth Company. until its sale in the early 1980s, it had more than 800 stores in the UK prior to closure.

Woolworths sold many goods and had its own Ladybird children's clothing range, Chad Valley toys, and Worth-It! value range.

The chain was the UK's largest buyer of Candyking "pick n mix" sweets. It was sometimes referred to as "Woolies" by the UK media, the general public, and occasionally in its own television commercials.

I always remember the Woolworths in Argyle st just over the road from Lewis's when I used to attend the college for printing and building at Georges sq, I used to go upstairs there to the Cafeteria at dinner time [lunch time some people may say but to most Glaswegians it was dinner time] It was always packed because the food was great and fairly cheap.

There seemed to be Woolworths shops spread all over Glasgow and they were always great value for money.

With its demise we had the £ shops take over from where "Woolies" shops used to be and yes you get good value in these shops but when Woolworths shops closed down for good it was like we were losing an auld Glasgow pal.

Bridge street subway station

Coming from the soo-side of Glasgow it's always amazed me that Bridge street subways station is so called ?, because it's in Eglinton street. Of course if you asked anyone where is Eglinton st subway station they would look at you as if you were daft.[only reason I can think of is because it was so near to Bridge st Railway station.

Irene [Donna] Robertson

A Jubilee in Summer.
That lasted seemed fur ever,
Doon the Green wae peeces,
Feedin ducks doon on the river,

Playin oan the swings fur hoors.
Till we feel aw seek and dizzy,
Dunns or Barrs ginger,
And Tizer that wiz fizzy.

Queues ootside the pictures,
Wae a man who wiz a singer,
Collecting aw oor coppers,
And danced and went his dinger.

Kai Ora fae the lassie,
Who selt stuff aff a tray,
A chock ice or some butterkist,
Tae watch King Kong wae Fay Wray.

Danny Gill

My first pint

I was 16 and a half years old and working out at Kilmarnock rd [out Giffnock way] I was a second year old apprentice bricklayer and was working alongside a young bricklayer called John Gardner aged 22, John actually came from Paisley and not only was he a good bricklayer but a great guy too.

He said to me one Friday night when we had been paid do you fancy a pint of beer son ? I said "Oh aye" so we had half hour to kill before the pubs opened [5 pm, this was 1964]. John and me got a bus to the Central station as that is where John caught his train to Paisley.

We went into the Buffet bar on the concourse and in here I tasted my very first pint of beer. Yippee I felt all grown up. John left my firm after about a year but I never forgot him for teaching me all the good tips about bricklaying and showing me where I had gone wrong without shouting at me and I always respected John for that.

Well we never met again and with me leaving Glasgow when I was 20 years old to live and work in other countries, I thought I would never ever see John again.

Then low and behold a friend of mine Ann-Marie Miller who is an arts school teacher and teaches in the Glasgow area got in touch with me through Facebook and said to me do you know a John Gardner!!!!

It appears that John was attending one of Anne-Marie's art classes and she asked him what did you work at before you retired and he answered as a bricklayer, she said I don't suppose you know a friend of mine who is also a bricklayer, his name is Danny Gill. John said yes I do and Anne-Marie said she nearly fainted.

I contacted John through Facebook and couldn't get over talking to him after an absence of 50 years I was gob-smacked.

This was about 3 years ago and yes on one of my yearly trips back to Glasgow on my holiday, I met up with John and we took a walk down memory lane.

I was meeting up with a rake of friends in the Clutha pub that day when I met John, actually he was standing outside the pub door having a smoke and I passed by him, when he said aren't you going to say hello Danny? I threw my arms around John and gave him a big hug.

Of course that day in the Clutha about 20 people had come to meet me and it was a great day meeting old friends and new friends. Unfortunately I was trying to speak to everyone so I never really had a chance to speak to John in depth. So we made a meet-up for three days later in the Square peg pub in St Enochs sq. What a brilliant day, we both told each other how we had got on in our lives, what an amazing meet-up with a real nice guy, I was over the moon as I never in my wildest dreams thought that I would ever meet up with Johnnie Gardner again in my life.

Thanks to Anne-Marie Miller and Facebook and of course my pal John who was the man to buy me my first ever pint of beer.

PS: Funny thing was that when I met up with my old bricklaying pal Jimmy O'Neill in Sydney Australia he was telling me about this bricklayer who taught him how to build fire-bricks but Jimmy never mastered it. [this was in England] With me talking to John it transpires that it was John that Jimmy was talking about , what a small world it is!!

Last night of the Trams

The tram system was gradually phased out between 1956 and 1962 (in favour of diesel-powered buses), with the final trams operating on 4 September 1962. By that time only one route remained in operation, the number nine which ran from Auchenshuggle to Dalmuir. On the final day of service there was a procession of 20 trams through the city, an event attended by 250,000 people. Apart from the Blackpool tramway, Glasgow became the last city or town in the UK to operate trams until the opening of the Manchester Metrolink in 1992.

In 1949 one tram line was converted to the Trolleybus operation. Thereafter Glasgow developed several trolleybus routes, but these were all replaced by diesel buses by 1967.

I remember as a 14 year old school boy standing at the bus stop on the last night of the Trams and remembered back to the times I had travelled on the "auld shooglie" Tram with my Ma. They had character about them and what always stuck in my mind was that when the Tram had reached its terminus the coductor/conductress pushed all the seats back to face the way that the Tram was now facing.

The Back court singer

In the days of the old tenements in Glasgow a regular occurrence was the singing voice coming up from the open back court, a poor soul standing there with his bunnet grasped in his hand and he was literally "singing for his supper". he would belt out "The Rose of Trallee" or "The Skye boat song" in the hope that a few old penny's would be thrown down to him or maybe if people never had money they would throw down a piece on jam to him. I always remember my Ma saying to me Danny son you never know what had happened to that man in his life, he could have had a family of his own and lost them or he could have been the best of men at one time but had now fallen on hard times. Remember "there but for the grace of God go I ". this man "The back court singer" was part of Glasgow history and I remember him well. Every area of Glasgow had their own back court singer singing in the open back court for their supper, God love them.

The Belt

Do you remember being at school and you got the "belt" from the teacher, worse still if it was "6 of the best" and sometimes you got the belt for nothing or the blackboard duster thrown at you. Thank God those days are over I think that some of those school teachers were sadists.

When I went to Holyrood senior secondary school I actually had Bob Crampsey [of STV's Scotsport fame] as one of my teachers and he very rarely ever gave you the belt, he would give you "Lines" instead. So he would say take 300 lines and give them to me tomorrow morning. Oh I hated "doing lines" because as soon as school was over all of us boys just wanted to play football in the street. Sometimes I wouldn't do my lines and in the morning at school before the 9 am bell rang I would pay my pals an old penny per one hundred lines so I could give the lines to Mr Crampsey who in turn wouldn't even look at them as he chucked them in the bin. I think I would actually have preferred the belt instead ha ha.

Joke

Back in the early 1960's this young lady brought her boyfriend back to her house to meet her father for the first time before heading off to the dance hall. Her father said to the young gentleman I bet you canny wait to "start screwing eh". The young guy went as red as a beetroot and his girlfriends father said oh don't be embarrassed son I know all you young folk are doing it all the time.

With that the young lady who had just walked into the room started screaming at her father How many times have I got to tell you its called "Twisting"!!!!

Glasgow Authors

There are so many Glasgow authors to choose from, covering different topics of reading and I have read quite a few of their books from Alistair McLean to Peter May etc, but I must say that I have started to read the books by Ian Todd.

They are called the "Glasgow Chronicles" but they were always sold as Kindle books [I'm a paperback book man myself] I had a look inside one of them and liked what I saw but wished that they were in paperback form.

Well they are now and I just finished the first one called "Parly rd" its all about the "Toon-heid" area where Ian was brought up and its written in "Glesga speak " its all about the local guys and the polis and everyone else. It will have you laughing but sad also sometimes as it depicts Glasgow at that era of the 60's - 70's. Have a look at them, they are on Amazon.

There are plenty of them so that's me fixed up after I have finished typing this book up.

Smog

I remember back in the 1950's we used to have terrible smog attacks, it was a combination of all the smoke belching form the tenement chimney's and factory chimneys and fog mixed together. It was that bad you could only see a couple of feet in front of you, in fact lots of people wore scarves over their mouths to stop inhaling this toxic stuff.

Some people who got a bus after work to go home would get off the bus and walk home as the bus only crawled along and they were actually quicker walking. Mind you it didn't stop all of us young street footballers playing our game even if we couldn't see where the ball was going . How was that for dedication.

I'm sure people of my generation remember these smog attacks, thank god a clean air act was passed in parliament stopping Factories using their chimneys and with the demolition of lots of the old tenements we started to use smokeless fuel like coke etc and by the early and mid 60's we were smog- free but I remember it like yesterday.

Fish and Chips

Fish and chips were Glasgow's first take away food service [before Chinese/Indian etc] and how we loved them. It seems on Friday nights most people had fish n chips from the local chippy. My job on these Friday nights were to go to the local chippy and queue up for two special fish suppers with plenty of salt and vinegar wrapped up in newspaper. To stop the fish n chips going cold on my way home I stuck them up my jumper to keep them warm. Oh the aroma of the fish and the smell of the salt n vinegar made me run as fast as I could back to out tenement and give them to my Ma. Then we all sat down round the kitchen table and savoured or Friday nights fish and chips. Pure magic.

Stair-head toilet

It seems most of us who lived in the tenements had to share the stair head toilet [some people were lucky to have an inside toilet and some even a bath] three different families all sharing the same toilet. When you walked down the stair to get there you always whistled and if someone was inside they would give a discreet cough so you either waited outside or if you were desperate run back up and use the emergency Po under the bed !!

We had the old fashioned cistern with the old chain hanging down and our toilet paper was wee squares of newspaper hanging down from the toilet wall tied with a piece of string or with a big nail through the middle of the newspaper to keep it in place. Changed days now when lots of us have heated toilets and en suite bathrooms.

Chapter 16

Poems

Lighting the Fire

I can remember all of those years ago, and yes God loves a trier.
A ritual duty of my generation was to daily light the tenement fire.

But before you could do this and I tell you sincerely I'm no kiddin.
Ye had to get last night's ashes and dump them all in the midden.

Then you'd hunker doon on your knees and the fire ritual began.
With a newspaper and kindling sticks at hand, this was the plan.

You'd build the sticks like a pyramid so the air cood pass through.
Scattering wee lumps of coal all around it, that is what I would do

Then you lit all the kindling sticks and slowly watch it all smoulder.
Bending doon and blowin air fae yer cheeks, tae the fire got bolder.

Then with your siblings standin watching you, their faces not glum.
A sheet of newspaper over the openin, it whooshed way up the Lum.

That was my generation , now sadly that fire-lighting skill has gone.
'Cos today to get some heat in the house, we jist turn the heating on

We will never ever forget that fire making ritual that we daily used to all go through will we. After getting the fire "going" we did what that lady above is doing and holding a sheet of newspaper over the fire opening to "draw the fire". Yes it always worked but the only drawback could be if you were not quick enough the newspaper could catch fire and as much as you tried to stop it, it flew up the chimney flue with a "Whoomp" or a "Whoosh". My job in the morning was to dump the last nights fire-ashes from the grate into the midden in the back court on my way to school. My Ma used to wrap the ashes up in a couple of sheets of newspaper and I had to hold my "parcel" close to my chest as I walked down the stair to the open back court. Of course you did get the occasional person who would open their tenement windae and chuck the wrapped up ashes onto the ground in the back court, when they landed the newspaper burst open and the ashes went everywhere but thank God not many people did this.I always remember one morning on my way to school that when I chucked the wrapped up ashes into the midden bin, I must have been standing too close to the midden because this blooming great big rat leaped out at me. I thought it was going for my "jugular". well I ran back up oor stair beating the Chris Chataway four minute mile record and my Ma said "have you forgotten something son". After getting my breathe back my Ma said well you'll no stand too close to the midden again in future wull you son, ha ha.

Porridge

You either loved it or loathed it and that's the honest truth.
Loving each spoonful of it or wantin to spit it oot yer mooth.

My sister sprinkled sugar over it I thought she'd never halt.
While I was totally opposite as over it I would sprinkle salt.

I used to sit and watch my Ma stirring Oats into that big pot.
As soon as she poured it into my plate I ate the bloomin lot.

Winter morning's the Porridge acted jist like central heating.
Weans that diddny eat Porridge had faces always greeting.

Summer months my Ma bought other cereals from the shop.
Either corn flakes or those wans that went snap/crackle/pop.

Got to say I wiz honestly glad Winter came back and nae fibs.
Cause Ma would make the Porridge that stuck fast to my ribs.

Ye can buy Porridge in packets into the micro wave it will go.
But it is not a patch on the stuff- Ma made all those years ago.

The stuff that sticks to your ribs eh, I used to sit and watch my Ma make it all those years ago, it really did start your day off well, it was our central heating, because the Glasgow winters when we were weans could be bloomin cold. Then it was off to school and your porridge kept you going until playtime. Of course at school we used to get a wee third of a pint bottle of milk in the classroom which I liked [some diddny] and our Ma always gave us our "Piece" usually a piece on jam which we devoured in seconds because we wanted to play football [boys] and for the lassies it was "beds" at school playtime. Here's a thing you might know or might not know but the expression your "Pieces" actually came from Porridge. What happened years ago was people would make porridge at night time and put it into a drawer and in the morning when it had "set" it was cut up into pieces. So when you say "your pieces" meaning a sandwich it actually derives from the "pieces of porridge" that were cut up in the morning and given to the men folk for their breaks at work. It's surprising but some everyday used words that we take for granted actually have a story behind them. Much similar to "going for the messages", years ago when there were no mobile phones or even TV to get the news. We used to go to the shops for food etc and we would meet up with other people/pals and we would exchange messages and pass them on to the next person we met, so this is how Messages came about.

The Square Sausage

Of aw the food I've ever eaten there's 1 that's my favourite meat.
People know it as the Lorne sausage, its so good it canny be beat.

Ye can have it with a full Scottish-breakfast a laying on your plate.
Beside yer egg, beans,tottie scone yir square sausage looks great.

I left Glasgow years ago to live in London with aw its cafe's galore.
But when I ask fur it on a crusty roll they hiddny heard of it before.

Aw the cafe owners said ,we hiv link sausages that taste so grand.
Well to be fair to them I tried them but the taste it was so bland.

World wide I've tasted all kind of sausages, but leave me at a loss.
Always dreamin of the square sausage aw covered in broon sauce.

Each year I holiday back in old Glasgow it's great to be back hame.
Leaving London far behind, their sausages jist dont taste the same.

Great ti be back with my ain folk and that is the God's honest truth.
Dying to eat a square sausage, that has me slavering at the mooth.

Yes our beloved Lorne sausage or as its commonly known to us Glaswegians as "the square sausage" when I tell some English people here in London they think I'm mad but then I show them it on facebook and they say maybe I'm not mad at all ha ha .Its part and parcel of our growing up in Glasgow and most of us I believe prefer broon sauce put on it. They started selling the square sausage here in London in the Iceland supermarkets and I bought some but it just doesn't taste the same. That's why when I get the train back to the Central station for London and as we pass by Carlisle I thing not long now and I always make a point of going into the Wetherspoons pub either beside Hope street or in Jamaica street and order a roll on square sausage and cover it in broon sauce. I always make a point of getting a slab of it to take back with me on my train journey back to the big smoke and put it in my freezer and lasts me for a week or two. People that have never tried it just don't know what they are missing eh. Another thing I like to do when devouring my square sausage in Glasgow when I'm on my holidays is to sit there and read the Daily Record or if its a Sunday then read the Sunday Post or Sunday Mail as the square sausage is being consumed and it really does make me feel back at Hame. Just sitting here in my flat in London typing this summing up of the square sausage on my computer has me bloomin slavering at the mooth. Lol.

The Swinging 60's--- Part 1

They say if ye remember the 60's, then you weren't really there
Well I can remember every year of it wae great music in the air

The Gorbals clearance had started, tenement's aw bit the dust
Dr No with Sean Connery at the cinema, to see 007 wiz a must

Hippy colonies in San Francisco aw into drugs of every manner
TV gave us Doctor Who, Coronation St gave to us Elsie Tanner

President Kennedy assassinated, part of me also died that day
America was still bombing Vietnam, wae its new President LBJ

Mary Quant and the Mini-skirt, fashions daft in Carnaby street
Sandie Shaw won the Eurovision song contest in her bare feet.

Scotland--3 England--2 at Wembley, Jim Baxter stole the Show
Celtic and Rangers both in European Finals , "Go Glasgow Go"

Jist a few events in the swinging 60's which ended far too soon
The highlight being of course, when man walked on the Moon.

Well folks this was surely the best decade ever [of course with some very sad events too]. I had just turned 13 years old in 1961 so I was at the very start of the swinging 60's. Oh the mini skirt how we men loved it. The Beatles were out of this world especially to me in their early years of 62-65. We were coming out of the austerity of World war 2 and to be young was brilliant, the whole music scene was so vibrant, then the Flower people and the Hippie movement came along. Of course terrible things were happening over in Vietnam and President Kennedy had been assassinated and the world grieved. Young people were starting to be heard and they had lots to say and were not going to be kept silent. The fashion scene went crazy especially in Carnaby st, later the "pill" made free love an open invitation and Sputniks were flying round the Moon with dogs and chimps inside them. Then the icing on the cake was when man walked on the Moon and we all held our breathe in anticipation of what would happen in the 70's. For me and being a teenager and starting to work and having money in the 60's was so brilliant. What a decade, too much to mention but absolutely fabulous.

241

Epilogue

Well folks that's us come to the end of my book and I hope you have enjoyed the reading about our Native Glasgow. I started with the intention of having lots more of peoples stories but as much as I asked for them I only got a few stories coming in which is fair enough as lots of people don't feel as if they're up to sending their story in. So what I had to do then was enlarge the other chapters to give the book a fair word and page count.

I have always believed that if you have around 200 pages in a book then that is not too bad, see it's not too long and not too short and with a 200 or so page count it feels comfortable in your hand as a paperback. [although lots of people nowadays prefer a kindle book]. Anything with a page count of under 140 pages I deem as too flimsy and less than a hundred pages is more or less like a pamphlet but there is no disrespect meant by me at all to these books and their Authors, as every book is the Authors pride and joy no matter how short or long. This is just my own personal view.

I sometimes pick a paperback book up and its 500 pages thick and before I even start to read it I'm put off with its thickness, so its all psychological really. So too short or too long can have an imprint on the reader even before they read the first page.

I have tried to put in as many different Topics and News bits to get general aspects put over to the reader and inserting Famous Glaswegians gave me lots of surprises as I researched them. Also as we all know there is a Green/Blue - - - Blue/Green divide in Glasgow , its been there since before I was born and will be there after I am no longer here on Earth but I never ran away from it as it is a part of our Glaswegian make-up, I'm not putting everyone into that category but I would say a high percentage of us are.

Myself I'm a Celtic supporter but I also have pals who are Rangers supporters so I have tried my best to be as even handed as I could be in my book and there is never any intention of me trying to belittle anyone for their football or Religious beliefs or any other belief or non-belief I have just tried to be fair in my input and here and there in some of the Chapters I have edited it to show no bias [best as I could]. Overall on that point I think I have done a fair job, if someone thinks not, then I tried my best is all I can say.

At the very start of my book and at the very end I have inserted a few poems but with a difference from poems inserted in my previous books.

In my previous books [but not my autobiography] I inserted poems at the beginning and end of my books with peoples stories and other aspects in the other chapters in between these poems.

This time though I thought that I would do something different and that is to first of all type the poem in on one page and on the opposite page have a photo of the poems subject which would relate to the reader immediately and the added bonus was to put text underneath the photo to give added information on the subject of the poem.

So I think overall I have given the reader a fair mix throughout the book to whet your appetite. Be it about Glasgow buildings or other etc.

On the point of housing schemes I wanted to go into detail about the upheaval of leaving our old tenement behind [for us who this happened to] and the frightening but perhaps exciting adventure that lay ahead in a new place which might have been on the other side of the Town, leaving family and life-long friends behind in this quest.
There are so many housing schemes all over Glasgow so what one did I opt for, actually I chose Castlemilk because a friend of mine Susan Casey and her friends wrote a book about Castlemilk and there is also the "The Big flit" which took a number of years to put together before it was published.

I asked her for her permission if I could put a summarised version of that book in Chapter 13 of my book, just showing what it was like where they lived before they moved to Castlemilk, the early days of settling in and the hardships they faced.

243

Of course this happened in all the housing schemes covering the greater Glasgow area so you actually could be talking about any new housing scheme back then. I know as the very same happened to my family when we moved to South Nitshill.

It has gave me great pleasure in doing the research for this book and I have found out a lot of things about Glasgow that I never knew before so I hope what I have written will enlighten you as much it did me.

Whether we stayed at home in Glasgow or travelled to the four corners of the Globe as many of us have done, we all have one thing in common and that is "We belong tae Glasgow".

Danny Gill
2019

Made in the USA
Monee, IL
17 December 2019